OPPOSING
VIEWPOINTS®
SERIES

Health Care

Other Books of Related Interest:

Opposing Viewpoints Series

Universal Health Care

At Issue Series

Health Care Legislation

Current Controversies Series

Health Care

> "Congress shall make no law ... abridging the freedom of speech, or of the press."

First Amendment to the US Constitution

The basic foundation of our democracy is the First Amendment guarantee of freedom of expression. The Opposing Viewpoints Series is dedicated to the concept of this basic freedom and the idea that it is more important to practice it than to enshrine it.

Health Care

David Haugen and Susan Musser, Book Editors

GREENHAVEN PRESS
A part of Gale, Cengage Learning

Detroit • New York • San Francisco • New Haven, Conn • Waterville, Maine • London

Elizabeth Des Chenes, *Managing Editor*

© 2012 Greenhaven Press, a part of Gale, Cengage Learning

For more information, contact:
Greenhaven Press
27500 Drake Rd.
Farmington Hills, MI 48331-3535
Or you can visit our Internet site at gale.cengage.com.

For product information and technology assistance, contact us at:

Gale Customer Support, 1-800-877-4253.
For permission to use material from this text or product, submit all requests online at www.cengage.com/permissions.

Further permissions questions can be emailed to permissionrequest@cengage.com.

Articles in Greenhaven Press anthologies are often edited for length to meet page requirements. In addition, original titles of these works are changed to clearly present the main thesis and to explicitly indicate the author's opinion. Every effort is made to ensure that Greenhaven Press accurately reflects the original intent of the authors. Every effort has been made to trace the owners of copyrighted material.

Cover image © mustafa deliormanli/iStockphoto.com.

LIBRARY OF CONGRESS CATALOGING-IN-PUBLICATION DATA

Health care / David Haugen and Susan Musser, book editors.
        p. cm. -- (Opposing viewpoints)
    Includes bibliographical references and index.
    ISBN 978-0-7377-5725-5 (hardback) -- ISBN 978-0-7377-5726-2 (pbk.)
    1. Medical care. 2. Medical policy. 3. Health care reform. I. Haugen, David M., 1969- II. Musser, Susan.
    RA393.H374 2012
    362.1--dc23

                                                                2011046481

Printed in the United States of America
1 2 3 4 5 6 7 16 15 14 13 12

Contents

Why Consider Opposing Viewpoints?

> "The only way in which a human being
> can make some approach to knowing
> the whole of a subject is by hearing
> what can be said about it by persons of
> every variety of opinion and studying
> all modes in which it can be looked at
> by every character of mind. No wise
> man ever acquired his wisdom in any
> mode but this."
>
> John Stuart Mill

In our media-intensive culture it is not difficult to find differing opinions. Thousands of newspapers and magazines and dozens of radio and television talk shows resound with differing points of view. The difficulty lies in deciding which opinion to agree with and which "experts" seem the most credible. The more inundated we become with differing opinions and claims, the more essential it is to hone critical reading and thinking skills to evaluate these ideas. Opposing Viewpoints books address this problem directly by presenting stimulating debates that can be used to enhance and teach these skills. The varied opinions contained in each book examine many different aspects of a single issue. While examining these conveniently edited opposing views, readers can develop critical thinking skills such as the ability to compare and contrast authors' credibility, facts, argumentation styles, use of persuasive techniques, and other stylistic tools. In short, the Opposing Viewpoints Series is an ideal way to attain the higher-level thinking and reading skills so essential in a culture of diverse and contradictory opinions.

In addition to providing a tool for critical thinking, Opposing Viewpoints books challenge readers to question their own strongly held opinions and assumptions. Most people form their opinions on the basis of upbringing, peer pressure, and personal, cultural, or professional bias. By reading carefully balanced opposing views, readers must directly confront new ideas as well as the opinions of those with whom they disagree. This is not to argue simplistically that everyone who reads opposing views will—or should—change his or her opinion. Instead, the series enhances readers' understanding of their own views by encouraging confrontation with opposing ideas. Careful examination of others' views can lead to the readers' understanding of the logical inconsistencies in their own opinions, perspective on why they hold an opinion, and the consideration of the possibility that their opinion requires further evaluation.

Evaluating Other Opinions

To ensure that this type of examination occurs, Opposing Viewpoints books present all types of opinions. Prominent spokespeople on different sides of each issue as well as well-known professionals from many disciplines challenge the reader. An additional goal of the series is to provide a forum for other, less known, or even unpopular viewpoints. The opinion of an ordinary person who has had to make the decision to cut off life support from a terminally ill relative, for example, may be just as valuable and provide just as much insight as a medical ethicist's professional opinion. The editors have two additional purposes in including these less known views. One, the editors encourage readers to respect others' opinions—even when not enhanced by professional credibility. It is only by reading or listening to and objectively evaluating others' ideas that one can determine whether they are worthy of consideration. Two, the inclusion of such viewpoints encourages the important critical thinking skill of objectively evaluating an author's credentials and bias. This evaluation will illuminate an author's reasons for taking a particular stance on an issue and will aid in readers' evaluation of the author's ideas.

It is our hope that these books will give readers a deeper understanding of the issues debated and an appreciation of the complexity of even seemingly simple issues when good and honest people disagree. This awareness is particularly important in a democratic society such as ours in which people enter into public debate to determine the common good. Those with whom one disagrees should not be regarded as enemies but rather as people whose views deserve careful examination and may shed light on one's own.

Thomas Jefferson once said that "difference of opinion leads to inquiry, and inquiry to truth." Jefferson, a broadly educated man, argued that "if a nation expects to be ignorant and free . . . it expects what never was and never will be." As individuals and as a nation, it is imperative that we consider the opinions of others and examine them with skill and discernment. The Opposing Viewpoints Series is intended to help readers achieve this goal.

David L. Bender and Bruno Leone,
Founders

Introduction

"Our predecessors understood that government could not, and should not, solve every problem. They understood that there are instances when the gains in security from government action are not worth the added constraints on our freedom. But they also understood that the danger of too much government is matched by the perils of too little."

Barack Obama, speech on health care, September 10, 2009.

"[Under the 2010 health care reform laws] the Administration will create mountains of regulations. . . . Health care will be politicized and made more cumbersome. The flexibility of providers and patients will be greatly reduced and creativity suppressed. Individual choice will be subordinated to decisions made by central authority. The regulations issued by the government will be grist for private litigation against providers and insurers."

John S. Hoff, Heritage Foundation Backgrounder #2459, September 10, 2010.

On March 23, 2010, President Barack Obama signed into law the Patient Protection and Affordable Care Act (PPACA). This massive piece of federal legislation attempts to curb costs of private and government health expenditures while expanding coverage to the country's uninsured. Supporters of the PPACA envision the legislation as a solution to looming crises in the health care field: namely, the rising price of care and the growing number of uninsured who either tap into health care resources they cannot afford or refrain from seeking care because of their lack of coverage. In a June 3, 2010, editorial for *The New England Journal of Medicine*, Jonathan Gruber cites statistics from the Centers for Medicare and Medicaid Services (CMS) that acknowledge that under the PPACA, costs for health care will still rise but by a far smaller percentage than if the system had not been reformed. He contends that PPACA-controlled growth will peak in 2016 with a 2 percent growth in expenditures. Gruber goes on to claim, "However, these increases are quite small relative to the gains in coverage under the new law. There are currently 220 million insured Americans, and the CMS predicts that 34 million more will be insured by 2019. The agency also estimates that without this reform, health care costs would grow by 6.6% per year between 2010 and 2019. So [under the PPACA] we'll be increasing the ranks of the insured by more than 15% at a cost that is less than one sixth of 1 year's growth in national health care expenditures." How exactly the government will cut expenditures is less certain, Gruber points out, but he believes the most obvious paths will be to reduce patient demand (by promoting preventative care, for example) and to make providers implement more cost-effective care (most likely through incentives and rewards).

Critics of the PPACA, however, insist that cost-cutting alone will not balance the health care budget. Some, like Curtis Dubay, a senior policy analyst for the Heritage Foundation, argue that the PPACA includes new taxes to generate income. He and other critics say that the new legislation seeks out individuals with high-premium health care plans and unfairly taxes them (a 40 percent excise tax on premiums beyond $23,000 for families and $8,500 for individuals). While supporters of the PPACA characterize such policyholders as Wall Street bigwigs who can afford the cost, others have shown that these plans are utilized by many middle-class union workers and employees of companies that happen to have better policies. Dubay also warns that the PPACA calls for new payroll income taxes and imposes a tax penalty on Americans who do not purchase health care. "Combined, all of these tax increases (including those on employers that do not provide health insurance for their employees and on individuals who do not buy health insurance) will cost taxpayers $503 billion between 2010 and 2019," Dubay attests in an April 14, 2010, post on the foundation's website.

For Dubay the imposing of taxes is clearly within the purview of government, and it can be opposed by legislators who believe that such taxes are unjust. More troubling though, for Dubay and other critics, is the penalty on those who do not wish to purchase health care. To subsidize the considerable array of proposed benefits, the PPACA will require each American (who can afford it) to buy health insurance even if he or she does not want any. Referred to as an individual mandate, this aspect of the new law seeks to compel Americans to purchase coverage under threat of penalty for noncompliance.

The architects of the law maintain that Congress has this authority under the US Constitution's Commerce Clause, a power given in Article 1, Section 8, which permits Congress to control economic activity (here, health care business) between states. However, on January 31, 2011, Judge Roger Vinson of the US District Court for the Northern District of Florida ruled against the individual mandate, claiming, "It would be a radical departure from existing case law to hold that Congress can regulate inactivity under the Commerce Clause." According to Vinson, the government could then compel citizens to make any other purchase lawmakers choose. "While the individual mandate was clearly 'necessary and essential' to the act as drafted, it is not 'necessary and essential' to health care reform in general," the judge argued; therefore he rejected the constitutionality of the entire law. Since Vinson's ruling, several states have challenged the constitutionality of the individual mandate.

Advocates of the PPACA are dismayed by this challenge, for they see the individual mandate as part of the foundation of health care reform. Most of these supporters attest that the individual mandate only seeks to make everyone pay their fair share of health care. According to Gruber, this time writing in an April 8, 2010, memo for the Center for American Progress, "Uninsured individuals impose major costs on the rest of society. These individuals do use medical care, and the latest estimates put the costs of uncompensated care at over $50 billion a year in unpaid medical bills." To counter these losses, the law holds people—for whom the cost of coverage would be less than 8 percent of their income—responsible for covering their expenses. Writing for CBS News's Money Watch on November 13, 2009, Mark Thoma explains that the insurance system only works efficiently and cost-effectively if the burden is borne by as many policyholders as possible. "Insurance must be distributed over a wide variety of people so that the average cost of care will be affordable," Thoma states. "One way to ensure that the pool is broad-based is to require that anyone who might need health care—i.e., everyone—purchase health insurance." If too many people use services without paying for them, then observers fear that the remaining health premiums will continue to skyrocket and employers will begin dropping plans because of the increasing expense.

Constitutional lawsuits against the current health care reform laws continue to mount, and popular opinion remains bitterly divided. In *Opposing Viewpoints: Health Care*, various experts and pundits examine the debates surrounding not only the passage of the Patient Protection and Affordable Care Act but the status of health care in the country and the direction of reform. In the chapters that follow, viewpoint authors acknowledge the problems posed by the uninsured and rising health care costs and debate the role of government in the health care system.

OPPOSING
VIEWPOINTS®
SERIES

CHAPTER 1

What Is the State of US Health Care?

Chapter Preface

When evaluating health care in the United States, experts often begin by defining exactly what the system is supposed to provide. Some assert the affordability of health insurance as a top priority; for others, it is quality of care. A few analysts, however, point out that in order to have either, accessibility is a crucial first step. For example, Kevin Pho, a physician and medical blogger, believes that rectifying the shortage of primary care doctors must occur before any other reform can be meaningful. "After all," writes Pho in a commentary for CNN on August 20, 2009, "what good is having health insurance if you can't find a doctor to see you?"

Pho illustrates his argument for improved access by using Massachusetts as a cautionary tale. Since the state's adoption of reform in 2006—which compels residents to buy health insurance or provides free coverage if their income is too low—nearly a half-million new patients who were previously uninsured are now flooding hospitals. Consequently the demand for medical services greatly outnumbers the pool of doctors. The current two-month waiting period to see a primary care physician has even led some patients to seek emergency room attention for routine procedures. The state budget now suffers from soaring costs due to the 7 percent increase in emergency room volume.

In commenting on the nation as a whole, Pho states that facilities under the Department of Veterans Affairs and Indian Health Services—two government-run health entities—also face a tremendous shortage of primary care physicians. Waiting periods have been reported as anywhere from one to six months. And for some with serious conditions, suggests Pho, that period can be detrimental.

The Patient Protection and Affordable Care Act (PPACA) of 2010—the core of today's current health care reform laws—is making efforts to reverse the shortage of primary care physicians by providing grants to train a new generation of primary care physicians. According to an April 2, 2010, article by Susan Jaffe, a writer for the *AARP Bulletin*, the government hopes to expand the number of general practice physicians by defraying costs of medical school for those that enter the field. It is also helping to fund general practice training programs at medical colleges. Jaffe reports that the PPACA is helping ensure quality care and access for Medicare and Medicaid patients by raising pay rates and ensuring bonuses for those primary care physicians who treat these patients. Yet Jaffe concludes by stating, "No one knows for sure whether bonuses and other changes will build up the supply of primary care doctors fast enough to keep pace with demand."

While medical schools are expected to increase their class sizes to accommodate the need for doctors, residency programs (the training grounds for new physicians) still take three to seven years to complete. Writing in the *Wall Street Journal* on January 4, 2010, physician Darrell G. Kirch reports that the US Department of Health and Human Services expects "overall demand for physician services will increase an estimated 22% between 2005 and 2020, while the number of primary care physicians will increase by only 18% during this period." Improving access, however, is only one promise of the PPACA. The authors in the following chapter debate this and other issues that impact the country's health care prognosis.

> "It is increasingly clear that the United
> States has nowhere near 'the best health
> care system in the world,' and that
> performance often falls markedly short
> of that of other countries."

The US Health Care System Is in Poor Shape

Karen Davis, Cathy Schoen, and Kristof Stremikis

Karen Davis is an economist and president of the Commonwealth Fund, a private organization devoted to analyzing and improving health care in order to influence public policy. Cathy Schoen is vice president of the organization, and Kristof Stremikis is a research assistant. The following viewpoint is an update to previous Commonwealth Fund reports (titled Mirror, Mirror on the Wall) *that have assessed the ranking of US health care alongside the health care systems and outcomes of other developed nations. In the viewpoint, Davis and her colleagues claim that survey data collected from these countries through select reports indicate that America's health care fares poorly in major areas including quality of care, access to care, efficiency, and general wellness.*

As you read, consider the following questions:

  1. In what aspect of "effective care" does the United States

Karen Davis, Cathy Schoen, and Kristof Stremikis, "Mirror, Mirror on the Wall: How the Performance of the US Health Care System Compares Internationally, 2010 Update," The Commonwealth Fund. Used by permission of The Commonwealth Fund.

perform well, according to Davis, Schoen, and Stremikis?

2. According to the survey results, what percent of US primary care physicians report getting relevant information back from specialists?

3. What percent of Americans with health problems said they were likely to have out-of-pocket costs of more than $1,000 for medical bills, according to the survey?

O ver the past decade, leaders in the United States have begun to realize that the nation's health care system is far more costly and does not produce demonstrably better results than any other system in the world. It is increasingly clear that the United States has nowhere near "the best health care system in the world," and that performance often falls markedly short of that of other countries. Despite this awareness, costs continue to accelerate relative to other countries. To do better, the U.S. must search for lessons that might be adopted or adapted to improve its system.

In the first major attempt to rank health care systems, the World Health Organization's (WHO) *World Health Report 2000* placed the U.S. health system 37th in the world. This called into question the value Americans receive for their investment in health care. The U.S. ranked 24th in terms of "health attainment," even lower (32nd) in terms of "equity of health outcomes" across its population, and lower still (54th) in terms of "fairness of financial contributions" toward health care. In the same report, the U.S. ranked first in terms of "patient responsiveness." Some experts have criticized the report's measures, methods, and data, including the fact that the data did not include information derived directly from patients.

Cross-national surveys of patients and their physicians offer a unique dimension that has been missing from international studies of health care system performance, including the WHO analysis. When such surveys include a common set of questions, they can overcome differences among national data systems and definitions that frustrate cross-national comparisons. Since 1998, The Commonwealth Fund has supported surveys about patients' and health professionals' experiences with their health care systems in Australia, Canada, New Zealand, the United Kingdom, and the United States. Germany and the Netherlands were added in 2005 and 2006, respectively, and are included in this analysis. Focusing on access to care, costs, and quality, these surveys allow assessments of important dimensions of health system performance. However, they have their own limitations. In addition to lacking clinical data on effectiveness of care and including data from a limited number of countries, the surveys focus on only a slice of the health care quality picture—patient and primary care physician perceptions of the care they received and administered.

While each of the seven developed countries in this study has a unique health system, they all face cost and quality issues. Comparing patient- and physician-reported experiences in these countries can inform the ongoing debate over how to make the U.S. health care system more effective and responsive to patient needs and also can be useful to the others in improving their own systems.

The Survey and Its Results

In 2005, The Commonwealth Fund established a Commission on a High Performance Health System to assess the overall performance of the U.S. health care system. In July 2008, the Commission released the second *National Scorecard on U.S. Health System Performance*, which ranked the nation's performance on 37 indicators, 11 of which were based on international comparisons. This report groups indicators into the same categories outlined in the Commission's *National Scorecard*, but uses a more extensive international database with 74 indicators drawing heavily on annual international surveys sponsored by The Commonwealth Fund. The five dimensions of high performance identified in the Commission's *National Scorecard* are: quality, access, efficiency, equity, and long, healthy, and productive lives. This report presents patients' and primary care physicians' views and an additional exhibit on health outcome measures, drawing on international comparisons reported in the Commission's *National Scorecard*. . . .

Overall, the U.S. ranks last or next-to-last on all five dimensions of a high performance health system, as it did in the 2007, 2006, and 2004 editions of *Mirror, Mirror*. Exhibit 1 provides a snapshot of how the seven nations rank on the domains of quality, access, efficiency, equity, and long, healthy, and productive lives. The Netherlands ranks first overall, scoring highest on access and equity. The United Kingdom, which ranks second overall, scores best of the seven countries in terms of efficiency. Australia ranks highest on long, healthy, and productive lives. New Zealand is first on quality of care. Canada and the U.S. rank sixth and seventh overall, respectively.

Quality Care

High-quality care is defined in the Commission's *National Scorecard* as care that is effective, safe, coordinated, and patient-centered. New Zealand ranks first and Canada last, based on averages of the scores in these four areas.

Effective Care In its discussion of effective care, the Commission's *National Scorecard* states that an important indicator of quality is the degree to which patients receive "services that are effective and appropriate for preventing or treating a given condition and controlling chronic illness." In this report, the indicators used to define effective care are grouped into two categories: prevention and chronic care (Exhibit 2).

Prevention: Preventive care is crucial to an effective health care delivery system. When utilized appropriately, lists of patients who are due or overdue for tests or preventive care, reminders

25

Health Care

Exhibit 1. Seven-Nation Summary Scores on Health System Performance

	AUS	CAN	GER	NETH	NZ	UK	US
OVERALL RANKING	3	6	4	1	5	2	7
Quality Care	4	7	5	2	1	3	6
Effective Care	2	7	6	3	5	1	4
Safe Care	6	5	3	1	4	2	7
Coordinated Care	4	5	7	2	1	3	6
Patient-Centered Care	2	5	3	6	1	7	4
Access	6.5	5	3	1	4	2	6.5
Cost-Related Access Problems	6	3.5	3.5	2	5	1	7
Timeliness of Care	6	7	2	1	3	4	5
Efficiency	2	6	5	3	4	1	7
Equity	4	5	3	1	6	2	7
Long, Healthy, and Productive Lives	1	2	3	4	5	6	7

TAKEN FROM: Karen Davis, Cathy Schoen, and Kristof Stremikis, "Mirror, Mirror on the Wall," June 2010.

Exhibit 2. Effective Care Measures

	Source	Raw Scores (Percent)							Ranking Scores						
		AUS	CAN	GER	NETH	NZ	UK	US	AUS	CAN	GER	NETH	NZ	UK	US
Overall Benchmark Ranking (with average of subcategories):									2	7	6	3	5	1	4
Prevention									2	7	6	5	3.5	3.5	1
Physicians reporting it is easy to print out a list of patients who are due or overdue for tests or preventive care	2009	63	18	37	65	57	90	24	3		5	2	4	1	6
Patients sent computerized reminder notices for preventive or follow-up care	2009	82	10	17	48	92	76	18	2	7	6	4	1	3	5
Receive reminders for preventive/follow-up care	2007	44	40	57	58	48	58	70	6	7	4	2.5	5	2.5	1
Doctor asked if emotional issues were affecting health	2007	37	36	25	27	31	25	46	2	3	6.5	5	4	6.5	1
Received advice from doctor on weight, nutrition, or exercise	2007	41	46	37	24	36	29	56	3	2	4	7	5	6	1

TAKEN FROM: Karen Davis, Cathy Schoen, and Kristof Stremikis, "Mirror, Mirror on the Wall," June 2010.

Exhibit 2. Effective Care Measures (continued)

	Source	Raw Scores (Percent)							Ranking Scores						
		AUS	CAN	GER	NETH	NZ	UK	US	AUS	CAN	GER	NETH	NZ	UK	US
Chronic Care									3	7	5	2	6	1	4
Diabetics receiving all four recommended services†	2008	36	39	40	59	55	67	43	7	6	5	2	3	1	4
Practice routinely uses written guidelines to treat diabetes	2009	87	82	77	98	93	96	82	4	5.5	7	1	3	2	5.5
Patients with hypertension who have had cholesterol checked in past year	2008	82	83	88	78	75	81	85	4	3	1	6	7	5	2
Practice routinely uses written guidelines to treat hypertension	2009	83	81	75	90	75	96	78	3	4	6.5	2	6.5	1	5
Practice routinely uses written guidelines to treat depression	2009	71	45	26	31	65	80	49	2	5	7	6	3	1	4

† Recommended services include hemoglobin A1c checked in past six months and feet examined, eye exam, and cholesterol checked in past year.

TAKEN FROM: Karen Davis, Cathy Schoen, and Kristof Stremikis, "Mirror, Mirror on the Wall," June 2010.

Exhibit 2. Effective Care Measures (continued)

	Source	Raw Scores (Percent)							Ranking Scores						
		AUS	CAN	GER	NETH	NZ	UK	US	AUS	CAN	GER	NETH	NZ	UK	US
Has chronic condition and did not follow recommended care or treatment plan because of cost	2007	11	7	0	1	9	10	24	6	3	1	2	4	5	7
Primary care practices that routinely provide patients with chronic diseases written instructions	2009	24	16	23	22	15	33	30	3	6	4	5	7	1	2
Physicians reporting it is easy to print out a list of patients by diagnosis	2009	61	34	68	67	56	97	41	4	7	2	3	5	1	6
Physicians reporting it is easy to print out a list of all medications taken by individual patients, including those prescribed by other doctors	2009	71	33	55	70	57	89	45	2	7	5	3	4	1	6

TAKEN FROM: Karen Davis, Cathy Schoen, and Kristof Stremikis, "Mirror, Mirror on the Wall," June 2010.

Exhibit 2. Effective Care Measures (continued)

	Raw Scores (Percent)								Ranking Scores							
Source	AUS	CAN	GER	NETH	NZ	UK	US		AUS	CAN	GER	NETH	NZ	UK	US
Doctor sometimes, rarely, or never reviewed all medications, including those prescribed by other doctors (base: taking prescriptions regularly)	2008	41	40	49	62	48	48	41		2.5	1	6	7	4.5	4.5	2.5

TAKEN FROM: Karen Davis, Cathy Schoen, and Kristof Stremikis, "Mirror, Mirror on the Wall," June 2010.

for preventive care visits, and discussions of emotional and lifestyle issues can increase the effectiveness of care through the early diagnosis or prevention of illness. Consistent with previous editions of *Mirror, Mirror*, the U.S. does especially well in providing preventive care for its population. Respondents in the U.S. were more likely than those in other countries to receive preventive care reminders and advice from their doctors on diet and exercise.

Chronic Care: Carefully managing the care of patients with chronic illnesses is another sign of an effective health care system. Overall, the U.K. outperforms the other countries on six of the 10 chronic care management indicators, while New Zealand and Canada lag behind. Different countries however, were successful on different aspects of chronic care. U.K. physicians are most likely to report it is easy to print out a list of all their patients by diagnosis. This finding may reflect the major push made by the U.K. government to implement health information technology (IT). Alternatively, low levels of IT use pull down the U.S. and Canada's scores. Germany does well on the percentage of hypertensive patients having their cholesterol checked and the extremely low percentage of patients with chronic conditions who do not follow recommended treatment or care because of cost.

The U.S. is fourth on effective care overall, performing well on prevention but average in comparison to other industrialized nations on quality chronic care management. The U.K. and Australia scored first and second place, respectively, in terms of effective care. The increased use of IT in the U.K. plays a large role in the country's high score on the chronic care management indicators, as well as its performance on system aspects of preventive care delivery. All countries, however, have room for improvement to ensure patients uniformly receive effective care.

Safe Care The Institute of Medicine describes safe care as "avoiding injuries to the patients from the care that is intended to help them." Sicker adults in Australia, Canada, and the U.S. reported the highest rates of medical and medication errors (Exhibit 3). Among those who had a lab test in the previous two years, sicker adults in the U.S. were more likely to have been given incorrect medication or experience delays in being notified about abnormal results. Canada, Germany, and the U.S. lag in terms of using IT to receive computerized alerts or prompts about potential problems with drug doses or interactions, with scores markedly below international leaders. Only 20 percent of physicians in Canada reported receiving such alerts compared with 95 percent in the Netherlands.

The U.S. ranks last out of the seven countries on safe care overall, while the Netherlands ranks first. Differences in education, cultural norms, and media attention, as well as the subjective nature of communication between doctors and patients might influence patients' perceptions of error. Therefore, caution must be used in relying only on patients' perceptions to rank safety. Nevertheless, these findings indicate that Americans, Australians, and Canadians have serious concerns about medical errors. Given the litigiousness of the population and concerns about personal costs of malpractice suits among physicians in the U.S., even perception of possible error has significance.

Coordinated Care In its discussion of coordinated care, the Commission's first *National Scorecard* report states, "Coordination of patient care throughout the course of treatment and across various sites of care helps to ensure appropriate follow-up treatment, minimize the risk of error, and prevent complications. . . . Failure to properly coordinate and integrate care raises the costs of treatment, undermines delivery of appropriate, effective care, and puts patients' safety at risk."

New Zealand ranks first among coordinated care measures, while Germany ranks last and the U.S. next-to-last (Exhibit 4). Chronically ill patients in the U.S. are least likely to report having a regular doctor (82%) while those in the Netherlands are

Exhibit 3. Safe Care Measures

	Source	Raw Scores (Percent)							Ranking Scores						
		AUS	CAN	GER	NETH	NZ	UK	US	AUS	CAN	GER	NETH	NZ	UK	US
Overall Benchmark Ranking									6	5	3	1	4	2	7
Believed a medical mistake was made in your treatment or care in past 2 years	2008	17	16	12	9	15	8	16	7	5.5	3	2	4	1	5.5
Given the wrong medication or wrong dose by a doctor, nurse, hospital, or pharmacist in past 2 years	2008	13	10	7	6	13	9	14	5.5	4	2	1	5.5	3	7
Given incorrect results for a diagnostic or lab test in past 2 years (base: had a lab test ordered in past 2 years)	2008	7	5	5	1	3	3	7	6.5	4.5	4.5	1	2.5	2.5	6.5
Experienced delays in being notified about abnormal test results in past 2 years (base: had a lab test ordered in past 2 years)	2008	13	12	5	5	10	8	16	6	5	1.5	1.5	4	3	7

TAKEN FROM: Karen Davis, Cathy Schoen, and Kristof Stremikis, "Mirror, Mirror on the Wall," June 2010.

Exhibit 3. Safe Care Measures (continued)

	Source	Raw Scores (Percent)							Ranking Scores						
		AUS	CAN	GER	NETH	NZ	UK	US	AUS	CAN	GER	NETH	NZ	UK	US
Hospitalized patients reporting infection in hospital	2008	7	6	6	5	11	10	7	4.5	2.5	2.5	1	7	6	4.5
Doctor routinely receives a computerized alert or prompt about a potential problem with drug dose or interaction	2009	92	20	24	95	90	93	37	3	7	6	1	4	2	5
Practice has no process for identifying adverse events and taking follow-up action	2009	15	55	48	68	15	5	31	2.5	6	5	7	2.5	1	4

TAKEN FROM: Karen Davis, Cathy Schoen, and Kristof Stremikis, "Mirror, Mirror on the Wall," June 2010.

Exhibit 4. Coordinated Care Measures

	Source	Raw Scores (Percent)							Ranking Scores						
		AUS	CAN	GER	NETH	NZ	UK	US	AUS	CAN	GER	NETH	NZ	UK	US
Overall Benchmark Ranking									4	5	7	2	1	3	6
Have a regular doctor	2008	89	92	97	99	95	92	82	6	4	2	1	3	4	7
Percent for whom specialist did not have information about medical history	2008	19	16	32	16	12	14	22	5	3.5	7	3.5	1	2	6
When primary care physicians refer a patient to a specialist, they always or often receive a report back with all relevant health information	2009	96	85	78	92	93	83	75	1	4	6	3	2	5	7
Percent of primary care physicians who report the amount of time they spend coordinating care for patients is a major problem	2009	17	33	29	20	18	20	30	1	7	5	3.5	2	3.5	6

TAKEN FROM: Karen Davis, Cathy Schoen, and Kristof Stremikis, "Mirror, Mirror on the Wall," June 2010.

Exhibit 4. Coordinated Care Measures (continued)

	Source	Raw Scores (Percent)							Ranking Scores						
		AUS	CAN	GER	NETH	NZ	UK	US	AUS	CAN	GER	NETH	NZ	UK	US
Doctor receives computerized alert or prompt to provide patients with test results	2009	68	12	11	8	41	49	22	1	5	6	7	3	2	4
Time was often or sometimes wasted because medical care was poorly organized	2008	26	29	31	21	23	18	36	4	5	6	2	3	1	7
Know whom to contact for questions about condition or treatment (among those hospitalized within past two years)	2008	83	88	88	85	85	80	92	6	2.5	2.5	4.5	4.5	7	1
Receive written plan for care after discharge (among those hospitalized within past two years)	2008	55	69	60	60	64	62	89	7	2	5.5	5.5	3	4	1

TAKEN FROM: Karen Davis, Cathy Schoen, and Kristof Stremikis, "Mirror, Mirror on the Wall," June 2010.

Exhibit 4. Coordinated Care Measures (continued)

		Raw Scores (Percent)								Ranking Scores						
	Source	AUS	CAN	GER	NETH	NZ	UK	US	AUS	CAN	GER	NETH	NZ	UK	US
Hospital made arrangements for follow-up visits with a doctor or other health care professional when leaving the hospital	2008	60	66	64	78	66	70	71	7	4.5	6	1	4.5	3	2
Percent of primary care physicians receive the information needed to manage a patient's care from the hospital in 2 weeks or less from when their patients were discharged	2009	89	63	81	87	96	75	82	2	7	5	3	1	6	4

TAKEN FROM: Karen Davis, Cathy Schoen, and Kristof Stremikis, "Mirror, Mirror on the Wall," June 2010.

most likely to have this connection (99%). Ninety-six percent of Australian primary care physicians report they always or often receive relevant information back from specialists, compared with 75 percent in the U.S. Only 17 percent of Australian physicians said the amount of time they spend coordinating care for patients is a major problem, roughly half the rate of those in the U.S. (30%) and Canada (33%).

Effective communication among patients, physicians, and hospitals is essential for high-quality care. Among chronically ill respondents who had been hospitalized within the past two years, American patients were the most likely to receive a written plan for care after discharge and to know whom to contact for questions about their condition or treatment when leaving the hospital. Seventy-one percent of American patients had arrangements for follow-up visits with a doctor or other health care professional made for them when leaving the hospital, second only to the Netherlands (78%). Physicians in New Zealand and Australia reported the highest rates of receiving information from the hospital needed to manage a patient's care within two weeks of discharge.

Patient-Centered Care The Commission defines patient-centeredness as "care delivered with the patient's needs and preferences in mind." The surveys explored issues related to provider-patient communication, physician continuity and feedback, and engagement and patient preferences. New Zealand ranked first and Australia second—although the two countries had fairly similar raw scores—among the group of seven countries with respect to engagement and patient preference, communication, and continuity and feedback measures. The U.S. was in the middle of the pack, ranking fourth (Exhibit 5). All countries could improve substantially in this area.

Communication: Communication measures included whether patients reported it was very or somewhat easy to contact

Exhibit 5. Patient-Centered Care Measures

	Raw Scores (Percent)								Ranking Scores						
	Source	AUS	CAN	GER	NETH	NZ	UK	US	AUS	CAN	GER	NETH	NZ	UK	US
Overall Benchmark Ranking									3	6	2	5	1	7	4
Communication									2	5	7	4	1	6	3
Patients reporting very or somewhat easy to contact doctor/GP's practice by telephone during regular business hours about a health problem	2007	83	75	45	77	89	81	79	2	6	7	5	1	3	4
Patients can communicate with regular place of care by email	2007	15	9	16	15	22	11	20	4.5	7	3	4.5	1	6	2
Doctor always explains things in a way you can understand	2007	79	75	71	71	80	71	70	2	3	5	5	1	5	7

TAKEN FROM: Karen Davis, Cathy Schoen, and Kristof Stremikis, "Mirror, Mirror on the Wall," June 2010.

Exhibit 5. Patient-Centered Care Measures (continued)

	Source	Raw Scores (Percent)							Ranking Scores						
		AUS	CAN	GER	NETH	NZ	UK	US	AUS	CAN	GER	NETH	NZ	UK	US
Received clear instructions about symptoms to watch for and when to seek further care when leaving the hospital (among those who had been hospitalized)	2008	74	79	70	75	71	72	87	4	2	7	3	6	5	1
Continuity and Feedback									**5**	**6**	**1**	**2.5**	**4**	**2.5**	**7**
With same doctor 5 years or more	2008	61	66	80	79	62	73	53	6	4	1	2	5	3	7
Doctor routinely receives and reviews data on patient satisfaction and experiences with care	2009	52	15	24	23	65	96	55	4	7	5	6	2	1	3
Regular doctor always knows important information about patient's medical history	2007	69	67	78	71	69	63	62	3.5	5	1	2	3.5	6	7

TAKEN FROM: Karen Davis, Cathy Schoen, and Kristof Stremikis, "Mirror, Mirror on the Wall," June 2010.

Exhibit 5. Patient-Centered Care Measures (continued)

	Raw Scores (Percent)							Ranking Scores						
Source	AUS	CAN	GER	NETH	NZ	UK	US	AUS	CAN	GER	NETH	NZ	UK	US
Engagement and Patient Preferences								4.5	4.5	3	6	1	7	2
Doctor always tells you about treatment options and involves you in decisions about the best treatment for you — 2007	66	62	62	60	67	54	61	2	3	4.5	6	1	7	4.5
Regular doctor always or often tells you about care, treatment choices and asks opinions — 2008	74	76	79	79	80	69	76	6	4.5	2.5	2.5	1	7	4.5
Regular doctor always or often encouraged you to ask questions — 2008	67	70	60	55	67	60	74	3.5	2	5.5	7	3.5	5.5	1
Regular doctor always or often gives clear instructions about symptoms, when to seek further care — 2008	79	77	81	75	79	69	80	3	5	1	6	3	7	2

TAKEN FROM: Karen Davis, Cathy Schoen, and Kristof Stremikis, "Mirror, Mirror on the Wall," June 2010.

a doctor's practice during regular business hours, whether they could communicate with their regular place of care by e-mail, and whether their doctor always explains things in a way they can understand. Patients who had been hospitalized were asked whether they had received clear instructions about what to watch for or when to seek further care. The U.S. ranked fourth in terms of the percentage of respondents who were able to contact the doctor's office by phone and ask about a health problem during regular business hours. The country did well relative to other nations on the measure of communicating by e-mail and had the best score on receiving clear instructions about further care when leaving the hospital. However, the U.S. was last on having doctors explain things in an understandable way.

Continuity and Feedback: The U.S. scores in the midrange on measures of continuity and feedback. Only slightly more than half (53%) of U.S. respondents had been with the same doctor for five years or more, compared with more than three-quarters (79%) of respondents in the Netherlands. The U.S. ranks third among the seven countries in terms of physicians routinely receiving data on patient satisfaction and experiences with care; 55 percent of American physicians receive such data. As in previous editions of this report, the U.K. continues to lead other nations in feedback: nearly all (96%) physicians in the U.K. receive patient satisfaction data.

Engagement and Patient Preferences: The surveys measured patient engagement by asking respondents whether their regular doctor always tells them about their options for care and asks their opinions; always or often encourages them to ask questions; or gives clear instructions about symptoms to watch for and when to seek treatment. While the U.S. set the benchmark in terms of doctors encouraging patients to ask questions, involvement in decision-making overall remains a problem for U.S. patients, as well as those in Canada, the Netherlands, and the U.K. As shown in Exhibit 5, the U.S. rank is average to poor on two of the four measures of patient engagement. New Zealand ranks highest on measures of being informed about treatment options and patients being asked for their opinion. German patients were most likely to receive clear instructions about symptoms and when to seek further care.

Access

Patients have good access to health care when they can obtain affordable care and receive attention in a timely manner. The 2007 and 2008 surveys included questions about whether patients were able to afford needed care (Exhibit 6). Specifically, respondents were asked if, because of cost, they did not fill prescriptions; get a recommended test, treatment, or follow-up care; or visit a doctor or clinic when they had a medical problem. The surveys also asked whether patients had serious problems paying medical bills and assessed out-of-pocket costs in each of the seven countries.

Cost-Related Access Problems The U.S. population continues to fare much worse than others surveyed in terms of going without needed care because of cost. Americans with health problems were the most likely to say they had access problems because of cost. More than half (54%) said they had problems getting a recommended test, treatment, or follow-up care; filling a prescription; or visiting a doctor or clinic when they had a medical problem because of cost. In the next-highest country, Australia, the comparable percentage was 36; patients in the Netherlands were the least likely to report having these problems (7%). Americans with health problems were significantly more likely to have out-of-pocket costs greater than $1,000 for medical bills (41%), as opposed to only 4 percent of adults in the U.K. Physicians in the U.S. acknowledge their patients have difficulty paying for care, with 58 percent believing affordability is a problem.

Timeliness of Care While the Netherlands ranks very highly on all measures of timeliness, different national patterns surface for

Exhibit 6. Access Measures

	Source	Raw Scores (Percent)							Ranking Scores						
		AUS	CAN	GER	NETH	NZ	UK	US	AUS	CAN	GER	NETH	NZ	UK	US
Overall Benchmark Ranking									6.5	5	3	1	4	2	6.5
Cost-Related Access Problems									6	3.5	3.5	2	5	1	7
Did not fill a prescription; skipped recommended medical test, treatment, or follow-up; or had a medical problem but did not visit doctor or clinic in the past 2 years, because of cost	2008	36	25	26	7	31	13	54	6	3	4	1	5	2	7
Patient had serious problems paying or was unable to pay medical bills	2007	8	4	4	5	8	1	19	5.5	2.5	2.5	4	5.5	1	7
Physicians think their patients often have difficulty paying for medications or out-of-pocket costs	2009	23	27	28	33	25	14	58	2	4	5	6	3	1	7

TAKEN FROM: Karen Davis, Cathy Schoen, and Kristof Stremikis, "Mirror, Mirror on the Wall," June 2010.

Exhibit 6. Access Measures (continued)

	Source	Raw Scores (Percent)							Ranking Scores						
		AUS	CAN	GER	NETH	NZ	UK	US	AUS	CAN	GER	NETH	NZ	UK	US
Out-of-pocket expenses for medical bills more than $1,000 in the past year, US $ equivalent	2008	25	20	13	8	14	4	41	6	5	3	2	4	1	7
Timeliness of Care									**6**	**7**	**2**	**1**	**3**	**4**	**5**
Last time needed medical attention had to wait 6 or more days for an appointment	2008	18	34	26	3	8	14	23	4	7	6	1	2	3	5
Percent of primary care practices who report almost all patients who request same- or next-day appointment can get one	2009	36	17	57	62	45	64	44	6	7	3	2	4	1	5
Primary care practices that have an arrangment where patients can be seen by a doctor or nurse if needed when the practice is closed, not including ER	2009	50	43	54	97	89	89	29	5	6	4	1	2.5	2.5	7

TAKEN FROM: Karen Davis, Cathy Schoen, and Kristof Stremikis, "Mirror, Mirror on the Wall," June 2010.

Exhibit 6. Access Measures (continued)

	Source	Raw Scores (Percent)							Ranking Scores						
		AUS	CAN	GER	NETH	NZ	UK	US	AUS	CAN	GER	NETH	NZ	UK	US
Somewhat or very difficult to get care on nights or weekends (base: sought care)	2008	62	56	35	30	39	44	60	7	5	2	1	3	4	6
Waiting time for emergency care was less than 1 hour (base: used an emergency room in past 2 years)	2007	54	38	73	73	61	50	52	4	7	1.5	1.5	3	6	5
Waiting time to see a specialist was less than 4 weeks (base: saw or needed to see a specialist in past two years)	2008	45	40	68	69	45	42	74	4.5	7	3	2	4.5	6	1
Waiting time of 4 months or more for elective/nonemergency surgery (base: those needing elective surgery in past year)	2007	18	27	5	7	13	30	8	5	6	1	2	4	7	3

TAKEN FROM: Karen Davis, Cathy Schoen, and Kristof Stremikis, "Mirror, Mirror on the Wall," June 2010.

the other countries in the study, depending on the particular health care service. Patients in the U.S. face financial burdens, but if insured, they have relatively rapid access to specialized health care services. The U.K. has relatively short waiting times for basic medical care and non-emergency access to services after hours, but has longer waiting times for specialist care and elective, non-emergency surgery. Conversely, a large number of German patients report waiting six or more days for an appointment the last time they needed medical care, yet the country has some of the shortest wait times for emergency care, specialist care, and elective, non-emergency surgery. Canada ranks last or next-to-last on almost all measures of timeliness of care. It is a common misconception to associate universal or near-universal coverage with long waiting times for care. That is not true either for meeting immediate care needs, as in the United Kingdom, or for specialist care—patients in Germany and the Netherlands have similar rapid access to specialists as U.S. patients.

Efficiency

In the Commission's first *National Scorecard* report, efficiency is described in the following way: "An efficient, high-value health care system seeks to maximize the quality of care and outcomes given the resources committed, while ensuring that additional investments yield net value over time." To measure efficiency, this report examines total national expenditures on health as a percent of gross domestic product (GDP), as well as the percent spent on health administration and insurance. An important indicator from the 2007 survey of adults includes whether patients spent any time on paperwork or disputes related to medical bills or health insurance.

Exhibit 7 also shows data from the 2008 survey on adults with health problems who visited the emergency department [ED] for a condition that could have been treated by a regular doctor had one been available, those whose medical records did not reach the doctor's office in time for an appointment, and

Exhibit 7. Efficiency Measures

		Raw Scores (Percent)							Ranking Scores						
	Source	AUS	CAN	GER	NETH	NZ	UK	US	AUS	CAN	GER	NETH	NZ	UK	US
Overall Benchmark Ranking									2	6	5	3	4	1	7
Total expenditures on health as a percent of GDP*	2007	8.9	10.1	10.4	9.8	9	8.4	16	2	5	6	4	3	1	7
Percentage of national health expenditures spent on health administration and insurance**	2007	2.6	3.6	5.3	5.2	7.4	3.4	7.1	1	3	5	4	7	2	6
Patient did not spend any time on paperwork or disputes related to medical bills or health insurance	2007	90	88	86	68	87	97	76	2	3	5	7	4	1	6
Visited ED for a condition that could have been treated by a regular doctor, had he/she been available	2008	17	23	6	6	8	8	19	5	7	1.5	1.5	3.5	3.5	6
Medical records/test results did not reach MD office in time for appointment, in past 2 years	2008	16	19	12	11	17	15	24	4	6	2	1	5	3	7

TAKEN FROM: Karen Davis, Cathy Schoen, and Kristof Stremikis, "Mirror, Mirror on the Wall," June 2010.

Exhibit 7. Efficiency Measures (continued)

	Source	Raw Scores (Percent)							Ranking Scores						
		AUS	CAN	GER	NETH	NZ	UK	US	AUS	CAN	GER	NETH	NZ	UK	US
Sent for duplicate tests by different health care professionals, in past 2 years	2008	12	11	18	4	10	7	20	5	4	6	1	3	2	7
Hospitalized patients went to ER or rehospitalized for complication after discharge	2008	11	17	9	17	11	10	18	3.5	5.5	1	5.5	3.5	2	7
Practice with high clinical information technology functions***	2009	91	14	36	54	92	89	26	2	7	5	4	1	3	6

* Data: OECD [Organisation for Economic Co-operation and Development], *OECD Health Data*, 2009 (Nov. 2009). Netherlands is estimated.

** Data: OECD, *OECD Health Data*, 2009 (Nov. 2009). Netherlands is estimated. U.K. data are from 1999.

*** Primary care practice has 9 to 14 of the following IT functions: EMR; EMR access to other doctors, outside offices, and patients; routine tasks, including ordering of tests and prescriptions and accessing test results and hospital records; computerized patient reminders, prescription alerts and tests results; "easy" generation of lists of patients by diagnosis, medications, needed tests, or preventive care. Significant differences between countries are indicated for distribution of summary variable rather than individual responses.

Health expenditures per capita figures are adjusted for differences in cost of living.

TAKEN FROM: Karen Davis, Cathy Schoen, and Kristof Stremikis, "Mirror, Mirror on the Wall," June 2010.

those who were sent for duplicate tests. It also reports on the incidence of hospitalized sicker adults who went to the emergency department or were re-hospitalized for complications during recovery. Indicators from the 2009 survey include primary care physicians' use of multidisciplinary teams and practices with high clinical IT functions. To be defined as a primary care practice with high clinical IT functionality, the practice must have or use nine of the following 14 tools: electronic medical records (EMRs); EMR access to other doctors, outside offices, and patients; routine tasks, including ordering tests and prescriptions and accessing test results and hospital records; computerized patient reminders, prescription alerts, and test results; easy generation of lists of patients by diagnosis, medications, needed tests, or preventive care.

On indicators of efficiency, the U.S. scores last overall with poor performance on the two measures of national health expenditures, as well as on measures of timely access to records and test results, duplicative tests, re-hospitalization, and physicians' use of IT. Of sicker respondents, those in Canada and the U.S. were most likely to visit the emergency department for a condition that could have been treated by a regular doctor had one been available, with rates three to four times that of Germany and the Netherlands. In the summary ranking, the U.K. scores first and the U.S. scores last.

Equity

The Institute of Medicine defines equity as "providing care that does not vary in quality because of personal characteristics such as gender, ethnicity, geographic location, and socioeconomic status." We grouped adults by two income categories: those who reported their incomes as above the country median and those who reported their incomes as below the country median. In all seven countries, adults reporting below-average incomes were more likely to report chronic health problems (not shown). Thus, reports from these lower-income adults provide particularly sensitive measures for how well each country performs in terms of meeting the needs of its most vulnerable population.

In Exhibit 8, we compare patient reports on various measures of access to care for adults reporting their incomes as below average and those reporting their incomes as above average. The rankings are based on the percentage-point difference between the responses of below-average income respondents to above-average income respondents, with a higher score indicating greater access problems for those with below-average incomes. We used survey measures expected to be sensitive to financial barriers to care, such as not getting needed or recommended care—including dental care—because of costs and difficulty getting care when needed.

The U.S. ranks low on all access to care measures and, as a result, does poorly on all measures of equity. Americans with below-average incomes were much more likely than their counterparts in other countries to report not visiting a physician when sick and not getting a recommended test, treatment, or follow-up care; not filling a prescription; or not seeing a dentist when needed because of costs. On each of these indicators, almost half of lower-income adults in the U.S. said they went without needed care because of costs in the past year.

In addition, Americans with below-average incomes were more likely than their counterparts in other countries to rate their doctor "fair" or "poor" and to have difficulty getting care in the evenings, on weekends, or on holidays. Below-average income respondents in Canada were more likely to report problems accessing timely care, including waiting more than one hour in the emergency department and waiting six days or more for a doctor's appointment. Among the higher-income population, U.S. respondents often were more likely than their counterparts in other countries to report difficulty obtaining needed care because of costs. That said, almost no U.S. respondents with above-average incomes rated their doctor "fair" or "poor," suggesting these Americans feel content in their choices of physician.

Exhibit 8. Equity Measures

Raw Scores (Percent):

	Source	Below-Average Income							Above-Average Income						
		AUS	CAN	GER	NETH	NZ	UK	US	AUS	CAN	GER	NETH	NZ	UK	US
Rated doctor fair/poor	2007	9	10	6	9	3	10	13	4	5	3	4	3	7	4
Had medical problem but did not visit doctor because of cost in the past year	2008	21	12	14	4	32	5	45	21	4	16	3	12	7	21
Did not get recommended test, treatment, or follow-up because of cost in the past year	2008	33	13	12	6	22	9	46	18	7	9	3	12	3	27
Did not fill prescription or skipped doses because of cost in the past year	2008	22	22	16	4	25	10	50	16	13	9	4	9	3	32
Needed dental care but did not see dentist because of cost in past year	2007	43	33	11	6	46	16	49	30	13	5	4	39	21	21

TAKEN FROM: Karen Davis, Cathy Schoen, and Kristof Stremikis, "Mirror, Mirror on the Wall," June 2010.

Exhibit 8. Equity Measures (continued)

	Source	Raw Scores (Percent):													
		Below-Average Income							Above-Average Income						
		AUS	CAN	GER	NETH	NZ	UK	US	AUS	CAN	GER	NETH	NZ	UK	US
Last time needed medical attention had to wait 6 or more days for an appointment	2008	21	36	27	2	6	14	28	18	25	21	3	5	15	15
Somewhat or very difficult to get care in the evenings, on weekends, or holidays (base: those who sought care)	2008	64	57	39	22	48	50	66	60	55	24	42	31	43	49
% waiting less than 1 hour in ER (base: those going to ER)	2007	46	38	70	82	56	54	47	59	36	78	70	62	52	57
Unnecessary duplication of medical tests in past 2 years	2008	12	11	19	3	10	6	21	15	9	15	5	6	4	18

TAKEN FROM: Karen Davis, Cathy Schoen, and Kristof Stremikis, "Mirror, Mirror on the Wall," June 2010.

Exhibit 8. Equity Measures (continued)

	Percentage-Point Difference Between Below-Average and Above-Average Income							Ranking Scores						
	AUS	CAN	GER	NETH	NZ	UK	US	AUS	CAN	GER	NETH	NZ	UK	US
Overall Ranking:								4	5	3	1	6	2	7
Rated doctor fair/poor	5	5	3	5	0	3	9	5	5	2.5	5	1	2.5	7
Had medical problem but did not visit doctor because of cost in the past year	0	8	-2	1	20	-2	24	3	5	1.5	4	6	1.5	7
Did not get recommended test, treatment, or follow-up because of cost in the past year	15	6	3	3	10	6	19	6	3.5	1.5	1.5	5	3.5	7
Did not fill prescription or skipped doses because of cost in the past year	6	9	7	0	16	7	18	2	5	3.5	1	6	3.5	7
Needed dental care but did not see dentist because of cost in past year	13	20	6	2	7	-5	28	5	6	3	2	4	1	7
Last time needed medical attention had to wait 6 or more days for an appointment	3	11	6	-1	1	-1	13	4	6	5	1.5	3	1.5	7

TAKEN FROM: Karen Davis, Cathy Schoen, and Kristof Stremikis, "Mirror, Mirror on the Wall," June 2010.

Exhibit 8. Equity Measures (continued)

	Percentage-Point Difference Between Below-Average and Above-Average Income							Ranking Scores						
	AUS	CAN	GER	NETH	NZ	UK	US	AUS	CAN	GER	NETH	NZ	UK	US
Somewhat or very difficult to get care in the evenings, on weekends, or holidays (base: those who sought care)	4	2	15	−20	17	7	17	3	2	5	1	6.5	4	6.5
% waiting less than 1 hour in ER (base: those going to ER)	−13	2	−8	12	−6	2	−10	7	2.5	5	1	4	2.5	6
Unnecessary duplication of medical tests in past 2 years	−3	2	4	−2	4	2	3	1	3.5	6.5	2	6.5	3.5	5

TAKEN FROM: Karen Davis, Cathy Schoen, and Kristof Stremikis, "Mirror, Mirror on the Wall," June 2010.

The Netherlands and the U.K. score highest on overall equity, with small differences between lower- and higher-income adults on most measures. Differences by income in Canada, Germany, and New Zealand most often emerged for services covered least well in universal national insurance programs, namely prescription drugs and dental care.

Cost-related access problems are particularly acute in the United States, where more than 46 million citizens are currently uninsured. Uninsured adults were more likely than insured adults to report difficulties getting needed care or going without care because of costs. However, differences by income persist even after taking insurance status into account. Compared with insured Americans with above-average incomes, insured Americans with below-average incomes were more likely to report going without care because of costs and difficulties seeing a specialist when needed. Compared with their counterparts in the six other countries, low-income Americans were significantly more likely to have access problems related to cost, even after controlling for health status and insurance.

Long, Healthy, and Productive Lives

The goal of a well-functioning health care system is to ensure that people lead long, healthy, and productive lives. To measure this dimension, the Commission's *National Scorecard* report includes outcome indicators such as mortality amenable to health care—that is, deaths that could have been prevented with timely and effective care; infant mortality; and healthy life expectancy.

Exhibit 9 summarizes country findings on each of these measures. Overall, Australia ranks highest, scoring in the top three on all indicators. It sets the standard with its scores on mortality amenable to health care and healthy life expectancy at age 60. The U.S. ranks last on mortality amenable to health care, last on infant mortality, and second-to-last on healthy life expectancy at age 60, although differences among countries are greatest on mortality amenable to health care.

Exhibit 9. Long, Healthy, and Productive Lives Measures

	Raw Scores								Ranking Scores						
	AUS	CAN	GER	NETH	NZ	UK	US		AUS	CAN	GER	NETH	NZ	UK	US
Overall Ranking									**1**	**2**	**3**	**4**	**5**	**6**	**7**
Mortality amenable to health care (deaths per 100,000)[a]	71	77	90	82	96	103	110		1	2	4	3	5	6	7
Infant mortality[b]	4.7	5	3.8	4.4	5.2	5	6.7		3	4.5	1	2	6	4.5	7
Healthy life expectancy at age 60 (average of women and men)[c]	24.6	23.8	23	22.8	23.7	22.5	22.6		1	2	4	5	3	7	6

[a] 2003 World Health Organization (WHO) mortality data.
[b] OECD, OECD Health Data, 2009 (Nov. 2009). Data are from 2006.
[c] World Health Statistics 2008, WHO Statistical Information System (WHOSIS). Data from 2006.

TAKEN FROM: Karen Davis, Cathy Schoen, and Kristof Stremikis, "Mirror, Mirror on the Wall," June 2010.

Overall Quality for Cost Is Leaking

This examination provides evidence of deficiencies in quality of care in the U.S. health system, as reflected by patients' and physicians' experiences. Although the U.S. spends more on health care than any other country and has the highest rate of specialist physicians per capita, survey findings indicate that from the patient's perspective, the quality of American health care is severely lacking. The nation's substantial investment in health care is not yielding returns in terms of public satisfaction.

> *"Despite serious challenges, such as escalating costs and care for the uninsured, the U.S. health care system compares favorably to those in other developed countries."*

The US Health Care System Is in Good Shape

Scott W. Atlas

In the following viewpoint, Scott W. Atlas refutes claims that the US health care system is inferior to those of other countries. Atlas maintains that Americans have better survival ratings for cancer, have access to preventative care, and spend less time waiting for care than patients in nations such as Canada and the United Kingdom. Atlas also points out that much of the world's health care innovations come from the United States, a leader in technological progress. Even though Americans still struggle with health care costs, Atlas argues that more government-run health care solutions—like those that dominate foreign health care systems—will not result in better care. Scott W. Atlas is a professor at the Stanford University Medical Center in Palo Alto, California, where he serves as a senior fellow at the Hoover Institution and a senior fellow at the Freeman-Spogli Institute for International Studies.

Scott W. Atlas, "Ten Reasons Why America's Health Care System Is in Better Condition than You Might Suppose," *Hoover Digest*, no. 3, 2009. Used by permission.

As you read, consider the following questions:
1. By what percent is death from breast cancer more prevalent in Canada than in the United States, as Atlas claims?
2. According to Atlas, how many British citizens are waiting for hospital admission or outpatient treatment at any
   given time?
3. As the author states, what percent of Americans reported
   being very satisfied with their health services?

Medical care in the United States is derided as miserable compared to health care systems in the rest of the devel-oped world. Economists, government officials, insurers, and aca-demics beat the drum for a far larger government role in health care. Much of the public assumes that their arguments are sound because the calls for change are so ubiquitous and the topic so complex. Before we turn to government as the solution, how-ever, we should consider some unheralded facts about America's health care system.

1. Americans have better survival rates than Europeans for common cancers. Breast cancer mortality is 52 percent higher in Germany than in the United States and 88 percent higher in the United Kingdom. Prostate cancer mortality is 604 percent higher in the United Kingdom and 457 percent higher in Norway. The mortality rate for colorectal cancer among British men and women is about 40 percent higher.

2. Americans have lower cancer mortality rates than Canadi-ans. Breast cancer mortality in Canada is 9 percent higher than in the United States, prostate cancer is 184 percent higher, and colon cancer among men is about 10 percent higher.

3. Americans have better access to treatment for chronic dis-eases than patients in other developed countries. Some 56 percent of Americans who could benefit from statin drugs, which reduce cholesterol and protect against heart disease, are taking them. By comparison, of those patients who could benefit from these

Long Wait Times in Canada

Despite a two week fall from the high reached in 2007, the total wait time [for hospital care in Canada] remains high [in 2009], both historically and internationally. Compared to 1993, the total waiting time in 2009 is 73 percent longer. Moreover, academic studies of waiting time have found that Canadians wait longer than Americans, Germans, and Swedes (sometimes) for cardiac care, although not as long as New Zealanders or the British.

Medical research has shown that longer waits can lead to adverse consequences for cardiac patients. Furthermore, economists attempting to quantify the cost of this waiting time have estimated it to amount to $1,100 to $5,600 annually per patient. . . .

The promise of the Canadian health care system is not being realized. On the contrary, a profusion of research reveals that cardiovascular surgery queues are routinely jumped by the famous and politically-connected, that suburban and rural residents confront barriers to access not encountered by their urban counterparts, and that low-income Canadians have less access to specialists, particularly cardiovascular ones, are less likely to utilize diagnostic imaging, and have lower cardiovascular and cancer survival rates than their higher-income neighbors.

Nadeem Esmail, "Waiting Your Turn:
Hospital Waiting Lists in Canada, 2009
Report," Fraser Institute, October 2009.
www.fraserinstitute.org.

drugs, only 36 percent of the Dutch, 29 percent of the Swiss, 26 percent of Germans, 23 percent of Britons, and 17 percent of Italians receive them.

4. Americans have better access to preventive cancer screening than Canadians. Take the proportion of the appropriate-age population groups who have received recommended tests for breast, cervical, prostate, and colon cancer:

- Nine out of ten middle-aged American women (89 percent) have had a mammogram, compared to fewer than three-fourths of Canadians (72 percent).
- Nearly all American women (96 percent) have had a Pap smear, compared to fewer than 90 percent of Canadians.
- More than half of American men (54 percent) have had a prostate-specific antigen (PSA) test, compared to fewer than one in six Canadians (16 percent).
- Nearly one-third of Americans (30 percent) have had a colonoscopy, compared with fewer than one in twenty Canadians (5 percent).

5. Lower-income Americans are in better health than comparable Canadians. Twice as many American seniors with below-median incomes self-report "excellent" health (11.7 percent) compared to Canadian seniors (5.8 percent). Conversely, white, young Canadian adults with below-median incomes are 20 percent more likely than lower-income Americans to describe their health as "fair or poor."

6. Americans spend less time waiting for care than patients in Canada and the United Kingdom. Canadian and British patients wait about twice as long—sometimes more than a year—to see a specialist, have elective surgery such as hip replacements, or get radiation treatment for cancer. All told, 827,429 people are waiting for some type of procedure in Canada. In Britain, nearly 1.8 million people are waiting for a hospital admission or outpatient treatment.

7. People in countries with more government control of health care are highly dissatisfied and believe reform is needed. More than 70 percent of German, Canadian, Australian, New Zealand, and British adults say their health system needs either "fundamental change" or "complete rebuilding."

8. Americans are more satisfied with the care they receive than Canadians. When asked about their own health care instead of the "health care system," more than half of Americans (51.3 percent) are very satisfied with their health care services, compared with only 41.5 percent of Canadians; a lower proportion of Americans are dissatisfied (6.8 percent) than Canadians (8.5 percent).

9. Americans have better access to important new technologies such as medical imaging than do patients in Canada or Britain. An overwhelming majority of leading American physicians identify computerized tomography (CT) and magnetic resonance imaging (MRI) as the most important medical innovations for improving patient care during the previous decade—even as economists and policy makers unfamiliar with actual medical practice decry these techniques as wasteful. The United States has thirty-four CT scanners per million Americans, compared to twelve in Canada and eight in Britain. The United States has almost twenty-seven MRI machines per million people compared to about six per million in Canada and Britain.

10. Americans are responsible for the vast majority of all health care innovations. The top five U.S. hospitals conduct more clinical trials than all the hospitals in any other developed country. Since the mid-1970s, the Nobel Prize in medicine or physiology has gone to U.S. residents more often than recipients from all other countries combined. In only five of the past thirty-four years did a scientist living in the United States not win or share in the prize. Most important recent medical innovations were developed in the United States.

Despite serious challenges, such as escalating costs and care for the uninsured, the U.S. health care system compares favorably to those in other developed countries.

> *"If current economic trends continue,*
> *more and more Americans will lose the*
> *health coverage they currently have."*

Many Americans Are Losing Health Insurance

Families USA

In the following viewpoint, Families USA, a nonprofit advocacy organization devoted to improving health care in the United States, claims that more and more Americans are losing their health coverage. Families USA maintains that the ranks of the uninsured are increasing due to high premiums, corporate decisions to terminate plans or cut back on coverage, and the growing unemployment problem. Prior to the passage of the Patient Protection and Affordable Care Act, the organization predicted the number of uninsured in the United States would rise above 50 million in 2010.

As you read, consider the following questions:

1. According to the Families USA findings, how many more people nationwide are losing health coverage each year?
2. By what percent did family health insurance premiums rise between 1999 and 2008, as Families USA claims?
3. According to Families USA, one in four non-elderly

"The Clock Is Ticking: More Americans Losing Health Coverage," Families USA, July 2009. www.familiesusa.org. Used by permission of Families USA.

Americans with health insurance in 2009 spent what percent of their pretax income on health care?

In this turbulent economy, Americans are not only losing their jobs and their homes—they are also losing their health coverage at an alarming rate. The latest data from the Census Bureau indicate that some 45.7 million Americans lacked health coverage in 2007, and economists believe that the situation has only worsened in the intervening months as the economic downturn has taken its toll.

Health reform is needed now more than ever. As health care costs rise, more and more families are priced out of health coverage. Increasing numbers of employers, especially small businesses, are no longer able to offer their employees affordable coverage, or in some cases, any coverage at all. If current economic trends continue, more and more Americans will lose the health coverage they currently have. National experts have predicted that at least 6.9 million more Americans will lose their health coverage by the end of 2010.

In this report, Families USA provides the first ever state-by-state illustration of the number of people who may lose health coverage between the beginning of 2008 (the period immediately after the last Census Bureau report on the number of uninsured) and the end of 2010 (the close of the current 111th Congress).

Projected Number of People Losing Health Coverage

With each passing week that meaningful health care reform is not enacted, more families in every state are losing health coverage:

- 44,230 more people are losing health coverage each week.
- 191,670 more people are losing health coverage each month.
- 2.3 million more people are losing health coverage each year.

Families USA based its state numbers on national estimates published in the peer-reviewed policy journal *Health Affairs* in May 2009. These estimates project that 6.9 million more Americans, primarily people in working families, will lose health coverage by the end of 2010. The *Health Affairs* analysis, which focused on the time period between 2008 and 2010, is based on a model that assumes that, during this time period, there will be no policy changes with respect to the health care system. It further assumes that personal income growth and per capita health spending among insured adults will follow the latest projections from the Congressional Budget Office and the Office of the Actuary at the Centers for Medicare and Medicaid Services (CMS), respectively.

This time period is appropriate for Families USA's analysis because it captures potential losses of coverage between the most recent Census Bureau calculations of the number of uninsured Americans (which reflect calendar year 2007) and the end of the 111th Congress (December 2010), which has taken up health reform as one of its major legislative goals.

In order to generate state-level numbers, Families USA calculated the share of uninsured, non-elderly individuals residing in each state using the most recent data reported in the Census Bureau's Current Population Survey for 2006–2007. We assumed that state losses in health coverage would parallel this distribution, and we apportioned the national estimate accordingly. The data suggest that the health care crisis is continuing to deepen across the nation, and that the longer Americans are forced to wait for health reform, the more people will lose coverage.

High Premiums Lead to Less Coverage

Over the last decade, health insurance premiums have risen at rates that far outpace inflation. Between 1999 and 2008, the average annual family premium more than doubled, soaring from $5,791 to $12,680, an increase of 119 percent. During the same time period, the Consumer Price Index, which measures infla-

Health Coverage Lost Between January 2008 and December 2010, by State

State	Average Number Losing Coverage			Total Number Losing Coverage, 2008–2010
	Per Week	Per Month	Per Year	
Alabama	590	2,550	30,570	91,710
Alaska	110	480	5,790	17,360
Arizona	1,180	5,120	61,430	184,280
Arkansas	470	2,030	24,330	72,980
California	6,380	27,640	331,730	995,200
Colorado	780	3,370	40,470	121,420
Connecticut	310	1,350	16,220	48,660
Delaware	100	420	5,010	15,030
District of Columbia	60	250	2,970	8,910
Florida	3,560	15,450	185,360	556,070
Georgia	1,590	6,890	82,720	248,160
Hawaii	100	420	5,050	15,160
Idaho	210	910	10,900	32,700
Illinois	1,660	7,180	86,200	258,600
Indiana	700	3,030	36,350	109,040
Iowa	280	1,220	14,600	43,800
Kansas	320	1,410	16,880	50,630
Kentucky	580	2,510	30,090	90,260
Louisiana	810	3,530	42,350	127,040
Maine	110	500	5,950	17,840
Maryland	740	3,190	38,260	114,780
Massachusetts	*	*	*	*
Michigan	1,040	4,500	54,030	162,100
Minnesota	430	1,880	22,580	67,750
Mississippi	550	2,370	28,390	85,180
Missouri	720	3,120	37,440	112,310
Montana	150	640	7,640	22,920
Nebraska	220	930	11,210	33,630

State	Average Number Losing Coverage			Total Number Losing Coverage, 2008–2010
	Per Week	Per Month	Per Year	
Nevada	450	1,940	23,310	69,940
New Hampshire	140	600	7,170	21,500
New Jersey	1,280	5,530	66,370	199,110
New Mexico	420	1,830	21,960	65,880
New York	2,470	10,720	128,580	385,750
North Carolina	1,480	6,420	77,000	230,990
North Dakota	70	290	3,420	10,260
Ohio	1,180	5,130	61,580	184,730
Oklahoma	620	2,690	32,240	96,730
Oregon	620	2,690	32,300	96,900
Pennsylvania	1,140	4,960	59,510	178,520
Rhode Island	100	420	5,050	15,160
South Carolina	670	2,910	34,920	104,750
South Dakota	80	360	4,280	12,850
Tennessee	810	3,520	42,290	126,880
Texas	5,550	24,070	288,860	866,580
Utah	370	1,620	19,480	58,450
Vermont	60	280	3,320	9,970
Virginia	1,020	4,410	52,900	158,700
Washington	710	3,070	36,850	110,540
West Virginia	240	1,040	12,490	37,480
Wisconsin	450	1,940	23,330	70,000
Wyoming	70	300	3,650	10,950
Total**	44,230	191,670	2,300,000	6,900,000

* Data for Massachusetts are not reportable because state-level data on the uninsured do not fully reflect changes in coverage under the Massachusetts health reform law, implementation of which began in 2006.
** Numbers do not add to total due to rounding, and because they do not include data for Massachusetts.

TAKEN FROM: Families USA, "The Clock is Ticking," July 2009. www .familiesusa.org.

tion, rose by only 29.2 percent. In the current economic downturn, working families are already struggling to afford basic necessities like groceries, car payments, gas, and housing costs. Paying for skyrocketing health care premiums is putting additional strain on families that are already financially strapped.

These high and continually rising premiums affect families as well as employers, and the combined result is that more and more Americans are losing health coverage. Employers that do continue to offer health coverage are being forced to pass on the rising costs to their employees by imposing higher premiums or copayments or by offering plans that cover fewer benefits. Other employers are choosing not to offer coverage at all because it is simply too expensive. Between 2000 and 2008, the share of firms offering health coverage declined by 6 percentage points, with small businesses being the most likely to drop coverage. Among firms with fewer than 200 employees that do not offer their employees health coverage, a total of 70 percent cited high premiums as either the most important reason (48 percent) or the second most important reason (22 percent) that they do not offer coverage.

Even if families are fortunate enough to have access to health coverage, either through job-based plans or through the individual market, they are still at great financial risk. In 2009, nearly one in four non-elderly Americans with insurance—53.2 million people—will spend more than 10 percent of their pre-tax income on health care. The problem is even worse for an estimated 14.3 million non-elderly Americans with insurance who will spend more than a quarter of their pre-tax income on health care in 2009. This financial burden means that some Americans are literally becoming impoverished in order to pay for health care costs.

When families are pushed to the brink by the current health care crisis, some must make tough choices between paying for health coverage and paying for other necessities, while others have no choice at all—they are simply forced to go without coverage.

A previous Families USA report found that during the two-year period from 2007–2008, an estimated 86.7 million Americans under the age of 65—one in three non-elderly Americans—were uninsured. The majority of these individuals (79.2 percent) were from working families where at least one family member was employed full- or part-time. These individuals either work for an employer that does not offer health coverage, or they cannot afford the coverage that is offered. The data presented in this report show that the number of people who find themselves in this situation is growing in every state.

Growing Unemployment Contributes to Further Coverage Losses

Since the data presented in this report are based primarily on working Americans, they do not account directly for the effect that growing unemployment is having on losses of health coverage. Nonetheless, with the economy in recession, rising unemployment is almost certainly fueling additional increases in the number of people who are losing coverage. The Urban Institute estimates that every 1 percent increase in the unemployment rate leads to a 0.59 percent increase in the number of adults under the age of 65 without health coverage. Between January 2008 and June 2009, unemployment swelled by 4.6 percent, so it is safe to assume that states will experience even greater losses of coverage between 2008 and 2010 than can be captured by our . . . findings.

The Trend Will Continue Unless Congress Enacts Reform

With each passing week, more Americans are losing their health coverage, and they will continue doing so if current economic patterns hold. Recent polling data show that Americans fear that instability in the availability and affordability of their health coverage will continue if health reform is not enacted. In order to stem the rising tide of uninsured in this country and to provide

American families with stable health coverage that they can depend on, Congress should act expeditiously to pass health reform legislation. As this report suggests, the longer Congress waits to enact meaningful health reform, the more American families will lose coverage in each and every state.

> *"For the young who don't luck into a job that offers coverage, a certain outlook becomes inevitable: Premiums are a fortune, you can barely pay your rent, you rarely need a doctor, [and] you decide to gamble."*

Many Americans Are Choosing to Live Without Health Insurance

David Amsden

In the following viewpoint, David Amsden, a writer for New York *magazine, reports on the prevalent attitude among many young Americans that they can forgo health insurance because they cannot afford the expense and they believe they are healthy. As Amsden states, many young people are employed in entry-level positions in firms that either do not offer coverage to that segment of their staff or simply do not provide coverage at all. Faced with other increasing costs of living—such as rent, food, and gas—young people bet against getting seriously ill or injured in order to stretch their budgets, Amsden points out. Without judging these "young invincibles," Amsden notes that when accidents or sudden illness occur, the out-of-pocket costs to the uninsured can be monumental enough to wipe out all savings and ruin credit ratings.*

David Amsden, "The Young Invincibles," *New York*, vol. 40, no. 11, April 2, 2007. Used by permission of The New York Magazine.

As you read, consider the following questions:

1. Why does Amsden say that many young people are entering into a world where "the old rules no longer apply"?
2. According to the Commonwealth Fund, as cited by Amsden, what percent of uninsured young adults say they have gone without health insurance because of the cost?
3. As Amsden describes it, what was the basic principle of the "landmark" health insurance plan Massachusetts passed in 2006?

It was an unfamiliar pain, sharp and persistent, as if a rag were being twisted inside his abdomen. Tighter and tighter, crunching in on his organs, enough to wake Andrew Ondrejcak one morning in 2004 before his alarm went off. Indigestion? No, probably it was a return of the stomach ulcers that had plagued him as an undergrad a few years back. Ulcers felt somewhat different, it's true, more an isolated stabbing compared with the lateral serrations currently tormenting him. But it had been a while; you forget the specifics of pain. Whatever it was, Ondrejcak, who was 24, worried he might have to see a doctor, something he made a point to avoid. Like 47 million other Americans, including most everyone he knew, Ondrejcak did not have health insurance.

Telling himself the pain was nothing, he walked to Sweet Melissa, a bakery on Court Street, where he made $6 an hour plus tips. He had come to New York from Mississippi, hoping to become a designer—maybe in theater, maybe fashion—but for the time being, he paid his rent (barely) by serving pastries. "Health insurance wasn't even an option," Ondrejcak told me. "I was flying through my savings, trying to get a career started. I was assisting designers who were doing great work, but I wasn't making anything. The last thing I'm going to do is spend $300 or whatever on insurance, you know?" He paused before adding, "I'm a healthy person, I rarely get sick. I run, I do yoga. I take all the vitamins. Honestly, I never thought about it."

At Sweet Melissa, the pain only worsened. But what to do? How to even *find* a doctor? Only one-third of the uninsured have a regular physician, and he was not among them. He searched the Yellow Pages for doctors in Brooklyn with the prefix *gastro* near their names; most wouldn't take him. Eventually, he found a public clinic—a friend had been there—that recommended a specialist in Bay Ridge. "It's probably ulcers," the doctor said, after Ondrejcak said *he* suspected ulcers. He was given a prescription for Nexium ($73) along with a depressing bill of $200 for the visit. "Basically all the money I'd made that week. I left keeling over in pain but took the bus home because I was so broke," he told me. He swallowed the Nexium with a swig of Maalox and went to bed, hoping the pill would rewire whatever was wrong.

Just before midnight, Ondrejcak woke in distress. Needling, jabbing, the pain was corrosive. "I crawled to my bathroom and tried to throw up because it hurt so bad," he recalled. "I was in my underwear on my bathroom floor calling my neighbor who had keys to my apartment." The neighbor phoned for a livery cab, asking the driver to take them to a hospital, any hospital, whichever was closest. Ten minutes later, Ondrejcak staggered into Long Island College Hospital in Brooklyn Heights. The desk attendant was blunt: No insurance? Wait in the emergency room. Ondrejcak had wondered about such a scenario—a sudden emergency, no safety net, the classic nightmare among the uninsured—but until now the thoughts were fleeting, theoretical. No way it would actually *happen*.

Betting Against Getting Sick

It's tempting to view a mindset like Ondrejcak's as purely a symptom of youth. The young are naturally resilient and among the least likely to have a serious medical condition—as far as priorities go, health insurance tends to reside in a muddled region of the mind along with other abstract concepts: retirement savings, mortgage payments, marriage, death. But this is only part of the story. Those coming of age today are entering an economy where many of the old rules no longer apply. The paternalistic corporate culture of the past (full-time staff members supported for the long haul) has been largely replaced by a frenetic "per-malance" model, the strivers and thrivers encouraged to jump from one company to the next as needed. There was a time when a health plan symbolized something—you were making it—but now benefits are scarce at many levels. For the young who don't luck into a job that offers coverage, a certain outlook becomes inevitable: Premiums are a fortune, you can barely pay your rent, you rarely need a doctor, [and] you decide to gamble. It's a state of mind so common, in fact, that the insurance industry has a name for it: Ondrejcak is one of the "young invincibles," those who, betting they can get through their twenties relatively un-scathed, "choose" to go without insurance. They are the fastest-growing segment of America's uninsured population.

There is, of course, a great deal of talk these days about health care. Open a newspaper and you'll find op-eds sermonizing about the coverage crisis, a poll dissecting public dissatisfaction, a study offering grim statistics ("Since 2000, the ranks of the un-insured have grown by 6.8 million") and yet another politician laying out a plan for universal care. Compared with small chil-dren, uninsured young workers are generally ineffective as politi-cal sympathy-generators and are therefore typically viewed as a footnote to the debate. But health-care analysts will tell you that insuring children, while certainly noble, is a relatively easy goal. "What a lot of people don't realize," says Peter Cunningham, a researcher at the Washington, D.C.-based Center for Studying Health System Change, "is that most children are already eligible for some form of care. They either qualify for Medicaid or can be insured under their parents' plan. So in many respects, it's a matter of making the paperwork clearer, not overhauling the sys-tem." The young invincibles, on the other hand, are an example of how the system bypasses some groups altogether. In this they are not alone—the poor have a long history of inadequate care, and increasingly, middle-class families are finding themselves priced out—though to understand their bind is to see just how ineffective the current system has become.

Balancing Health Coverage Against Other Pressing Costs of Living

"People tend to trivialize the issue," says Karen Davis, president of the Commonwealth Fund, a research foundation that recently published a comprehensive report on uninsured young adults.

> The most common misperception is that they're pretty healthy all in all and end up getting decent care without insurance. Yes, when you're injured in an accident, you won't be left in the street. But getting good rehab? That may not be an option. Most of the uninsured aren't getting regular Pap smears, they skip tests and treatments, they tend to end up in the emergency room because they wait until the last possible minute—they are developing unhealthy habits that are likely to stick with them as they grow up and start having more-serious health problems.

New York, unsurprisingly, is an especially fertile breeding ground for the uninsured young. "A lot of the professions that draw young people to New York—everything from retail to the arts to restaurants to software development—tend to have spottier coverage," says James R. Tallon, the president of the United Hospital Fund, a health-care think tank. Even large corporations are increasingly reluctant to offer coverage. (At a company like MTV, for instance, many full-time employees work in a nebulous state of hourly wages and no benefits, an arrangement that can last years.) Those without employer-sponsored coverage are thrown into a market where individual premiums can cost anywhere from $250 (for a bare-bones catastrophic policy) to $900 a month, among the highest rates in the nation, and likely out of reach for someone just starting out. And so going without health coverage becomes one of those casual sacrifices that come with being young in New York—on par with funneling half your income into a 400-square-foot apartment.

As an informal litmus test, I recently sent an e-mail to a handful of people in their twenties asking three vague questions: Are you uninsured? Know someone who is? How has it affected your life? Forward it to anyone, I encouraged. I imagined I would get a fair number of replies—one in four New Yorkers is uninsured, so I wasn't exactly shooting in the dark, and as a 27-year-old former young invincible myself, I had an undoubtedly skewed sample—but I was unprepared for the sheer volume of response: more than 100 replies within a couple of days, mostly from people I had never met. There were complaints, conspiracy theories, details of unpaid debts, stories of untreated injuries, shoddy care, one insurance-inspired marriage (he needed surgery), and, in the case of a musician friend, wisdom teeth that should have been pulled years ago. The messages led to interviews with more than 50 uninsured New Yorkers. If there was a dominant theme to these conversations, it was that being uninsured has a distinct way of tweaking one's perception of the city: New York becomes a kind of phobia-forming obstacle course, one navigated with the goal of keeping doctors at bay.

Nichole Schulze, a 31-year-old former publicist and current student at the Fashion Institute of Technology, was quick to rattle off a battery of quasi-logical preventive measures: "You won't see me snowboarding or mountain biking or even jaywalking. My friends think I'm a freak because I'm the only person in New York who actually waits until the light changes to cross the street. Oh, and I eat a kiwi every morning because I read somewhere that they contain twice the vitamin C of oranges. And if it's snowing? I'm the one walking on the inside of the sidewalk, just in case a cab decides to swerve and hop the curb." Should any of these methods fail? "I carry an expired Blue Cross card in my wallet. You never know, maybe they'll think I have insurance and I'll get better care."

Andrew Kuo, a 29-year-old painter, told me he made a vow to be insured by the time he turned 30. "But that was when 30 seemed like a ways away," he added. "Now I find myself making all these stupid calculations. Like, it would cost me around $3,000 a year to have insurance, right? Okay, isn't that about what it would cost out of pocket if I broke my wrist? Chances are I'm not going to break my wrist once a year, so why not save the money for that one-time emergency?" Like many I spoke with, Kuo said he'd happily pay for insurance, if only the cost-benefit analysis tilted more in its favor. "What's ironic is that I would never live without my cell phone, but I won't consider buying health insurance. It sounds ridiculous to say that out loud, but the fact is insurance is just too expensive. If it was the same price as my phone"—$150 a month sounded reasonable to him—"I'd buy it in a second."

Age Banding to Attract Young Consumers

The common assumption is that the exorbitant rates are schemed up by the politically influential executives governing the trillion-dollar insurance industry. But if insurers could target cheaper plans at younger New Yorkers, they would: Every business thrives by exploiting untapped markets. State law, however, requires insurers to follow a "community rating" system that throws everyone—young, old, sick, healthy—into one risk pool. "The whole point of insurance is that you're pooling the risk to spread out the costs for everyone," explains Cunningham. "If you target healthier groups with favorable policies, you're likely going to make it more expensive for the older, less-healthy populations who need regular care." Of course, if the young and healthy don't buy policies at all, who's balancing the costs? Recognizing this Catch-22, some states have adopted a more flexible "age banding" system, allowing insurers to customize packages based on age. WellPoint recently created a youth-centric program called Tonik, with plans as low as $67 a month, but it's currently only available in eight states.

According to the Commonwealth Fund report, nearly 60 percent of uninsured young adults (ages 19 to 29) say they have gone without health care because of the cost. Deny the symptoms until they vanish: Such becomes the standard protocol, supplemented by a regimen of self-diagnosis and self-treatment. Trent MacNamara, a 27-year-old fact-checker at *GQ*, was riding his bike down lower Fifth Avenue last year when the door of a garbage truck opened in his path, knocking him off his bike and into the middle of the road, where the Jeep Cherokee behind him ran over his forearm. MacNamara was wearing a helmet and remained conscious; remarkably, no bones were broken. "Once I realized I was more or less all right, the first thing that went through my head was that I didn't have insurance," he told me. "When the paramedics arrived, I pleaded with them to let me go. I kept asking if they thought I had broken ribs, and they kept saying they weren't qualified. Finally, they told me that if I could breathe without pain, they probably weren't broken. I promised them I would walk to the hospital. I just limped to the subway and went home." . . .

Substandard Care for the Uninsured

At the emergency room of Long Island College Hospital, Andrew Ondrejcak explained the nature of his stomach pain to an intern. Notes were taken. The intern vanished. This happened three times in five hours. At 7 A.M., nearly seven hours after he arrived, Ondrejcak was given a CT scan. "Within fifteen minutes of getting the results back, I was on the operating table, opened up," he said. "Apparently, my appendix was about to rupture."

What took so long? Appendicitis is among the easiest conditions to diagnose: A CT scan will detect it 90 percent of the time, and appendectomies are among the most common surgeries performed. But CT scans are expensive, and doctors, when dealing with the uninsured, are hyperconscious of burdening both patient and hospital with undue expenses. According to a report by the Institute of Medicine, the uninsured are far more likely to receive inadequate care in hospitals: Conditions are improperly managed; most bleakly, the uninsured are more likely to die in hospitals than the insured. "It's those catastrophe situations where insurance really proves invaluable," says the United Hospital Fund's James Tallon. "Without insurance, you're likely going to run into a roadblock at every stage of the process. Will you get a referral? Will you get the right tests? What kind of care are you going to get?"

After Ondrejcak came out of surgery, his mother arrived from Mississippi and noticed something the nurses had somehow overlooked: Her son was sweating profusely, yet his skin was cold to the touch, and a rash had broken out over most of his upper body. "My mom is typically this very sweet southern woman, but she was so pissed off," he recalled. "She asked if I was getting negligent care because I didn't have insurance. Later, the doctor made some remark about how the hospital is 'careful' with cases like mine because most people never pay." It turned out that Ondrejcak was having an allergic reaction to the antibiotics, so he was taken off the medicine. The rash subsided, but the healing process was jeopardized. The following night he was discharged, only to find himself in serious pain again four days later—a condition the surgeon initially diagnosed as the result of an "idle mind." "He said I'd been sitting around all day, and that sometimes your mind can believe things are happening that aren't really happening," remembered Ondrejcak. "I couldn't believe it."

When his test results came back, the doctor's tone was more urgent. Ondrejcak's white-blood-cell count was three times normal, his pain likely connected to an internal infection and not at all imagined. He was ordered to come to the hospital "immediately," a term that has a different meaning to the uninsured. Once again, Ondrejcak had to be admitted via the emergency room, wait a few hours, then explain to the ER physician that his doctor had sent him, wait while they paged the doctor, and again before being admitted. He spent the next three days in the hospital, getting injections of intensive antibiotics every eight hours.

At last, he started to heal properly. Three weeks later, the only evidence of the ordeal was a two-inch-long burgundy-colored scar below his right hipbone.

"And then," said Ondrejcak, "I got the bills."

They came separately, over the course of a week. The most damaging expenses were for his overnight stays: $16,608.76 for his first, $16,223.61 for the second. Then came the surgeon's bill ($1,665.50), the anesthesiologist's ($1,014), the two ER physicians ($605), the blood clinic ($551), and the post-op clinic ($592.04). A staggering $37,259.91 in total, a sum far higher than the pre-negotiated rates the hospital would have charged an insurer. "That's one of the unfortunate ironies," says Cunningham. "The same people who don't have insurance because they can't afford it are charged much higher rates than someone with insurance."

Panicking, Ondrejcak called the hospital. "Look, I have no money," he told the woman from billing. "What am I supposed to do?"

Incurring Debt for Unpaid Medical Bills

Debt is a condition that can plague the uninsured long after they've recovered from whatever brought it on in the first place. Nearly half of all uninsured young adults have problems trying to pay off bills—taking second and third jobs, being hounded by collection agencies. Some analysts have noted the oppressive effect this can have on the economy at large: Debt pigeonholes the young into unwanted jobs, slowing down the overall job market. "The debt itself is devastating," says Commonwealth's Karen Davis. "Credit histories are ruined—it takes years, sometimes lifetimes, to come out from under it." . . .

Debt isn't simply a problem for the uninsured who incur it; unpaid medical bills reverberate through the whole system. "It filters down to the rest of society," explains Cunningham. "Either the hospitals or the physicians absorb the cost, making the funding streams less certain and their capacity to deliver services more constrained. And premiums for everyone else go up." This point has become a favorite among those advocating a system overhaul. "We, in essence, have become the insurers of the un- insured," Victor Campbell, then-chairman of the Federation of American Hospitals, said last month [February 2007] when un- veiling a proposal for universal coverage. And in January, when Arnold Schwarzenegger announced that he would make insur- ing every Californian the cornerstone of his second term as gov- ernor, he sold the plan by stressing the "hidden tax" paid by the insured to offset the debt created by the uninsured. As a stopgap measure to prevent the cycle of debt and higher costs from spiral- ing even more out of control, a handful of states have proposed raising the age under which children remain eligible to receive care under their parents' plans. (In New Jersey, those as old as 30 now qualify.) Massachusetts has gone the furthest, passing a landmark plan to make health insurance like car insurance: le- gally required and relatively affordable. Yet for all the reform on a state level, analysts note that states don't have the revenue to sustain these programs for the long term. As Cunningham puts it: "Eventually, the federal government will have to step in and figure out a way to make it all work."

Facing nearly $40,000 in medical bills, Ondrejcak pleaded with the hospital. The only thing he could do, they told him, was apply for Medicaid assistance. He sorted through bank state- ments and pay stubs and submitted his claim: His documented income for the month of the surgery came to $507. (He didn't include tips or off-the-books work.) A paltry sum, especially by New York standards. And yet a few weeks later he received a let- ter from Medicaid denying his request. The limit for assistance was an even paltrier $352.10. How was he expected to pay nearly $40,000 because he made $1,800 a year too much? File for an appeal, the hospital suggested. On October 13, 2004, Ondrejcak presented his case at the Medicaid Assistance Program on West 34th Street. "It was all very cut-and-dry," he said. "Me, a woman representing Medicaid, and a judge-type guy. She was like, 'I'm sorry, there's nothing I can do,' and the other guy gives me a look like, 'Dude, you're fucked.' We all agreed in this itty-bitty room that there was nothing they could do to help me, but they all knew I was going to leave $40,000 in debt."

Notes from creditors began appearing in his mailbox, and Ondrejcak grew desperate. "Here's the deal," he told the hospital. "I'm either going to file for bankruptcy, which will ruin my credit and ensure that you'll never get any money, or I'm going to look into a malpractice lawsuit." On March 20, 2005, almost exactly a year after the surgery, he received a letter stating that his hospital costs had been reduced—by 100 percent. The other doctors followed suit, offering substantial discounts, and in the end, Ondrejcak had to pay only $1,700. It was an extraordinary conclusion for him, but a common one for hospitals. When the sums are so high that a payment plan isn't feasible, hospitals are often forced to simply write off the treatment as a loss. New York hospitals alone provide $1.8 billion in uncompensated care annually.

The Invincible Attitude Prevails

It has been just over a year since Ondrejcak paid his last medical bill. Now 27, he no longer works at Sweet Melissa, having established himself as a freelance set designer for fashion shows. He works in a studio near the Gowanus Canal that he shares with a client, the designers behind the trendy Vena Cava line. A sun-speckled loft with wide-plank flooring, white-brick walls, and exposed air shafts, it's a space that epitomizes a kind of bohemian success: independent, informal, [and] productive. During one of our meetings, he was in the process of conceptualizing Alice Roi's Bryant Park show, one of a handful he was working on for Fashion Week, and had to excuse himself numerous times to give assistants direction or to answer calls from his agency. His circumstances are vastly different from the morning he woke up in pain—on the surface, at least. "My credit is basically destroyed," he said. "It's amazing how much it haunts you. The other day, I tried to apply for an extension on my credit limit and they rejected it, bringing all this up. I can't even imagine what will happen if I ever, like, try to buy a house."

Toward the end of one of our conversations, I asked Ondrejcak, the least invincible of young invincibles, how coming down with appendicitis changed his attitude toward health insurance. Did he now see it as essential? Given what he had been through, and that he was better off financially, I assumed the answer was obvious. I was wrong. "Oh, no, I still don't have any insurance," he told me, rolling his eyes to indicate that, yes, he knows how it sounds. "I think about it, but it's not like I have a consistent income right now. I think about paying $300 a month on top of my other expenses, and it's like, *God, when's it going to end?*" He paused. "But, really, it's more than that. I was just so disillusioned with the process. I wanted nothing to do with it, you know? And maybe because, in the end, I kind of managed to get away with it, I end up thinking. . ." He trailed off, not finishing the thought, but the sentiment was clear: He is still young, he runs, he does yoga, [and] he takes all the vitamins. And it's not like you can get appendicitis twice.

> "With its one-two punch of rising health
> care costs and more seniors to cover,
> Medicare will eat up more and more of
> the federal budget in the years ahead."

Medicare Is Unsustainable and May Bankrupt the Nation

David Nather

A former writer for Congressional Quarterly, David Nather continues to contribute columns to news sources covering congressional issues. He is also the author of The New Health Care System: Everything You Need to Know. *In the viewpoint that follows, Nather argues that most experts are in agreement that Medicare costs are ballooning, ensuring that this health care safety net for US seniors will consume more and more of the federal budget in coming years. Nather contends that the Barack Obama administration's new health care law was designed to limit Medicare's growth without sacrificing its entitlements, but he worries that the spending cuts may not be deep enough and that Congress may undo parts of the law that provide the most savings. Nather also warns that congressional leaders are not fond of backing Medicare cuts for fear of backlash from seniors, so he shows equal concern that Congress will fail to unite behind needed cuts or will adopt less*

David Nather, "Medicare: An Entitlement out of Control," iWatch News, November 7, 2010. www.iwatchnews.org. Used by permission.

effective measures that will trim some costs but not arrest the big spending problems.

As you read, consider the following questions:

1. In what period of time does Nather believe Medicare might consume more of the federal budget than Social Security?

2. Since 2002 how many times has Congress stalled proposed cuts to doctors' fees, according to the author?

3. As Nather writes, what is the Independent Payment Advisory Board set up under the new health care law, and how did Congress immediately seek to limit the board's power?

If Congress had known in 1965 how expensive Medicare would become, it might not have approved the program in the first place. So Lyndon Johnson made sure it didn't know.

He railed against his budget advisers for trying to predict the long-term costs. "The fools had to go projecting it down the road five or six years," he complained to Sen. Edward M. Kennedy at the time. Johnson's allies were getting nervous, according to historians David Blumenthal and James Morone, so Johnson had to hide the price tag.

And when Wilbur Mills, then the chairman of the House Ways and Means Committee, worried about how much cash would be needed to cover doctor's services, Johnson was happy to throw more money into the mix. "Tell Wilbur that 400 million's not going to separate us friends when it's for health," Johnson said.

Forty-five years later, the costs of the Medicare program have become all too obvious. Medicare is a significant part of the reason the national debt is soaring out of control. It is an indispensable safety net for millions of senior citizens and people with disabilities, who depend on it to protect them from bankrupting medical bills. But since it's an open-ended program—with no upper limit—the nation has no similar protection to keep Medicare from bankrupting the country. The way things are going, Medicare could do just that.

Medicare Is Consuming More and More of the Budget

With its one-two punch of rising health care costs and more seniors to cover, Medicare will eat up more and more of the federal budget in the years ahead. But it's also politically untouchable. When either Democrats or Republicans try to suggest ways to trim the costs, they're accused of trying to push Grandma down the stairs in her wheelchair. Republicans did it to the Democrats during the debate over the new health care law, and Democrats are doing it now, at the height of election season, as Republicans float their own proposals.

Medicare is already growing faster than Social Security, and it could become bigger and more expensive than Social Security in the next 25 years. It is also growing faster than the economy, and if that keeps up, Medicare could cause the national debt to swell up to more than two-thirds of the gross domestic product in just the next decade.

For years, experts have also warned that Medicare faces trillions of dollars in unfunded liabilities—meaning that it will have to pay trillions of dollars more than the amount of money that is coming in. In fact, last year, the Medicare trustees warned that the program was facing more than $36 trillion in unfunded obligations.

Facing the Problem

This year [2010], the Medicare trustees said that problem has basically disappeared because of spending cuts in the new health care law. But critics in Congress and the federal government—including Medicare's chief actuary—don't buy it. They believe those rosy projections come from playing games with the math.

"It's a completely unsustainable system," said Republican Rep. Paul Ryan of Wisconsin, who could become the next chairman of the House Budget Committee if the Republicans win control of the House in November [2010]. The United States would still have to spend trillions of dollars to maintain the program as it is, Ryan said, "and we can't do that without bankrupting the country and shutting down the economy."

The future of Medicare is not just a partisan concern. "I understand the importance of Medicare in people's lives. I've seen it in my own family," Sen. Kent Conrad of North Dakota, the Democratic chairman of the Senate Budget Committee, said at a January hearing. "But the suggestion that we don't have to do anything is just not being straight with people."

Medicare also provides a vivid and alarming window into why America's entire health care system is so expensive. Nationally, health care experts believe that as much as a third of all health care spending—about $800 billion a year—goes to health care that doesn't make us better. That's happening for reasons that affect all health care, but since Medicare accounts for more than one fifth of all personal health care spending, its payment policies have a massive impact on what happens in the rest of the system.

The big challenge, not just in Medicare but in all of our health care spending, is to figure out how to bring the costs down without taking away needed care. That's why it's so important to make sure Medicare is spending its money wisely.

Unfortunately, the system as it exists today often does exactly the opposite. An analysis of Medicare claims data that was obtained jointly by the Center for Public Integrity and *The Wall Street Journal* reveals how Medicare is paying millions of dollars for procedures and services that, based on available evidence, don't really make sick people better. In an upcoming series of stories, the Center will demonstrate how a portion of that spending has been powered by a medical industrial complex of equipment-makers, pharmaceutical firms and specialists that have manipulated the system to increase Medicare payments and benefit their bottom lines, instead of patients.

The new health care law President [Barack] Obama signed in March was supposed to put the brakes on some Medicare spending by establishing pilot programs to address these issues. But no one knows if these experiments will work, or if they do, whether they'll be sustained. Many of the Medicare cuts might be overturned anyway if politically powerful health care providers complain too much about them.

Despite the rhetoric, the administration and Congress have a lot more work to do to steer Medicare's spending toward the most effective care, rather than a fee-for-service system that benefits doctors—especially specialists—more than patients. The nation's budget picture will only get better if Medicare becomes smarter about where and how it spends its money. "It's a very big factor, and the passage of health care reform didn't do much to change that," said Robert Bixby, executive director of the Concord Coalition, an organization that pushes for changes to the nation's entitlement programs to reduce growing budget deficits.

But all of the protests over the new health care law are only going to make it harder—not easier—to bring Medicare spending under control. Remember all of the raucous town hall protests and the charges of "rationing" and "death panels"? Just wait until Congress tries something that really puts a lid on Medicare spending. The program simply can't go on like this—but no one can get it under control without getting shouted down.

Huge Benefits, Massive Costs

Lyndon Johnson may not have considered $400 million a lot of money for Medicare, but now there's a lot more than $400 million being thrown around. This year alone, Medicare will spend some $451 billion—about 12 percent of all federal outlays.

By the standards Medicare was supposed to meet, it is an incredible success story. This year, 47 million Americans will get their health coverage through the program—mostly senior citizens who wouldn't be able to afford medical care or get decent insurance otherwise. The program pays for medical care for 39 million seniors and 8 million people under age 65 who have permanent disabilities.

"The enactment of Medicare assured access to health care for millions of Americans age 65 and over, and prevented millions from being forced into poverty," said John Rother, executive vice president of policy and strategy for AARP [an advocacy group formerly known as the American Association of Retired Persons]. Before Medicare, he said, "when you got into retirement age, you were on your own."

But at the rate it's growing, Medicare is also pushing the national debt to frightening levels.

Right now, the national debt is a little more than half the size of America's gross domestic product [GDP], and it could grow to as much as two thirds of GDP in just 10 years. And Medicare's spending is growing faster than the economy. If Medicare's spending isn't slowed down substantially, the debt could become even larger, according to the Congressional Budget Office.

Medicare isn't the biggest of the open-ended entitlement programs, which have to give benefits to everyone who qualifies. That title still belongs to Social Security. But Medicare's price tag is growing faster than Social Security's. Right now, Medicare is about 3.6 percent of the size of the national economy, compared to 4.8 percent for Social Security. By 2035—twenty-five years from now—Medicare will be 5.9 percent, almost as large as Social Security.

And that's actually the best-case scenario. It's only going to happen that way if Congress doesn't block a series of cuts in Medicare payments to doctors and other health care providers that are supposed to happen over the next 10 years.

Potential Congressional Interference

But Congress isn't exactly known for showing that kind of discipline. Payments to doctors are already supposed to be slashed deeply from their current levels, thanks to a 1997 law that calls for yearly payment cuts to strengthen Medicare's finances. But Congress keeps delaying the cuts, and put off a scheduled 21 percent decrease just this summer; the longer lawmakers stall on this, the deeper the eventual proposed cuts will get.

And starting next year, the new health care law is supposed to raise the fees for other providers at less than the rate of inflation, a change that is supposed to push them to become more productive. Over the next 10 years, that adjustment is supposed to save $157 billion.

The cuts were one of the chief mechanisms that allowed Congress to pay for the new health care law. But, of course, Congress has a history of stopping these kinds of cuts before they take place—just as it has been putting off the changes that are supposed to lead to the cuts in doctors' fees. In fact, Congress has stalled those cuts 10 times in the last eight years. If it delays those changes again and cancels the other provider payment cuts in the new law, Medicare will swell to 7 percent of the size of the national economy in 2035—larger than Social Security.

In their most recent report, issued in August, the Medicare trustees said the program should be in better financial shape under the new law. They said the trust fund for hospital expenses should now last until 2029, rather than running out in 2017, and that Medicare's coverage of physician services should be more stable as well. But Bixby and other critics have faulted the trustees for assuming the Medicare savings will help the program's finances, when they're actually being used to pay for other health coverage expansions under the law. The trustees also warned that they had to tie their estimates to "unrealistic substantial reductions in physician payments."

And in an unusually harsh statement, Richard S. Foster, the chief actuary of the Medicare program, said the report's projections "do not represent a reasonable expectation for actual program operations" because providers won't be able to cut their costs enough to match the cuts in their payments. "The best available evidence indicates that most health care providers cannot improve their productivity to this degree—or even approach such a level," Foster wrote, and "Congress would have to intervene to prevent the withdrawal of providers from the Medicare market and the severe problems with beneficiary access to care that would result."

As Bixby put it, "He went about as far as a civil servant can go in saying, 'Congress pulled a fast one here.'"

Why Costs Are Growing

Medicare is under financial stress because two powerful forces are combining to push spending higher and higher. The first force: changing demographics. Because of the aging of the population, driven by the large cohort of baby boomers, Medicare is expected to cover as many as 79 million people in 20 years—nearly twice as many as it covers now.

That's a problem unique to Medicare, but the other force is the same one that is bedeviling all of health care: rising costs for each person. Over the last 40 years, average annual health care spending has grown faster than the economy by anywhere from 1.3 to 3 percentage points each decade. The overall spending trends are a bigger factor in Medicare's budget pressures than the growth in the elderly population, according to Tricia Neuman, vice president of the Henry J. Kaiser Family Foundation and director of its Medicare project.

Why is that? State-of-the-art medical technology gets part of the blame. A host of new medical equipment can treat conditions that couldn't be treated before, but they're not designed to save money, and it's so profitable for health care providers to stock up on expensive gadgets like CT and MRI scanners. That drives as much as half to two-thirds of all growth in health care spending.

Some new medical procedures do save money and are less invasive than the old ones, but they still drive overall spending up because so many more people get them. Chronic conditions are also a crucial factor in rising costs—especially in Medicare, where they may account for as much as a third of all spending growth in recent years.

But the big problem that may explain why health care spending is so much higher in some places than others—without any evidence that the patients do better because of it—is that doctors have too many incentives to give patients more and more care, rather than better care. As long as they get paid for each medical service they give their patients, they have little reason to ask whether a test or procedure is really necessary.

In an influential article in *The New Yorker* last year, author and surgeon Atul Gawande compared the practice of medicine in two Texas towns, McAllen and El Paso, to find out why McAllen spends so much more on its health care even though the demographics are about the same in both places. He found that McAllen had lots of doctors who owned surgical or imaging centers and used them to bring in revenue. McAllen didn't have better care. It just had more of it.

The problem isn't just that health care providers are paid to perform too many services. It's that specialists are rewarded more than the primary care physicians who are likely to be needed in coming years. Robert A. Berenson, a senior fellow at the Urban Institute, studied Medicare's payment rates and found that radiologists, surgeons, cardiologists and dermatologists earn more per hour than the primary care physicians who perform important, basic services. The same is true for private health insurance, which often takes its cues from Medicare.

Specialists are "not the doctors who will be up in the middle of the night helping you with a crisis," said Berenson. "People want to go into them [specialty practices] because of the lifestyle, but they're also the most lucrative."

Small Fixes Will Not Solve the Problem

There are plenty of ideas on how to cut back spending without taking away urgently needed care. But there's not much evidence yet on which of those ideas work best. So the heftiest cuts the new law will make to Medicare spending have nothing to do with the root causes of the out-of-control spending growth.

The cuts in payments to providers, for example, are a major portion of the law's Medicare savings. But fee cuts will do nothing to stop the overuse of services—and there's no guarantee that Congress won't just get cold feet and cancel the cuts anyway.

Another considerable source of savings—$136 billion over 10 years—comes from lowering the payments to some Medicare Advantage plans, private plans that deliver Medicare services. Those plans are being targeted because Democrats in Congress say they get too much money from the federal government. But going after wasteful private plans isn't the same thing as tackling the broader incentives to overuse medical services.

The new health care law does set up a series of experiments with newer approaches that health care experts believe might actually change the equation. For example, different groups of providers will be able to join together to form "accountable care organizations," in which they can work together across different settings, try to save money for the Medicare program, and keep some of what they save. In addition, there will be a five-year pilot program that directs Medicare to give providers "bundled" reimbursement—a single payment that covers an "episode of care," such as surgery and follow-up care.

There will also be a new agency—the Center for Medicare and Medicaid Innovation—to guide other experimental approaches, such as coordinating medical care more carefully for people with chronic conditions and paying physicians salaries instead of separate fees for each action.

All of these initiatives have a common goal: to change the culture of medicine so health care providers are paid for providing the best care, not just more of it. The experiments could make a difference, some health care analysts say, but only if lawmakers and federal officials give them a chance to prove themselves—a big "if."

"It's going to be important that Congress is supportive of a creative and aggressive strategy, and they've got to realize that there will be some failures as we learn what works," said Gail Wilensky, a former administrator of the agency that runs Medicare, now known as the Centers for Medicare and Medicaid Services. Unfortunately, Wilensky said, the agency's culture has traditionally not tolerated failures in pilot programs. And if there are no failures in the new round of experiments, she said, "You know you're not being very creative or imaginative." . . .

Useful Care vs. Wasteful Care

There's also going to be more federal support for research that looks at two or more different ways of treating a medical condition to see which one works the best. The term of art is "comparative effectiveness research," and it's the feature that provoked many of the charges that the new law would lead to rationing. After all, who wants a bunch of government bureaucrats telling you that you can get one kind of medical care but not the other?

The real point, though, is to give medical providers a better idea of what's useful and what's wasteful. Medicare will be able to use the research to make some decisions on what to cover and what not to cover—sort of. Congress wrote in multiple restrictions to prevent some tough decisions that might feel scary. For example, the research can't be the only factor in the coverage decisions, and the Medicare program won't be able to make those decisions in a way that values the lives of elderly, disabled, or terminally ill people any less than other people's lives.

But if the program couldn't use the research at all, Medicare officials would have no real way to encourage the most effective medical services—so it would just keep paying for the wasteful or ineffective ones. "If we're steering people toward the interventions that work best," said Rother of AARP, "that's not rationing. That's improving the productivity of health care."

The new health care law also creates the Independent Payment Advisory Board, a 15-member expert panel that will recommend ways to cut back on Medicare spending, starting in 2014, if the program's costs grow too fast. The cuts it recommends will take place automatically unless Congress approves a different set of cuts that save the same amount of money.

The idea was to let an outside board make the politically unpopular cuts that Congress refuses to make. But lawmakers' fear of "rationing" caused them to enact substantial limits on what the board could actually do. For one thing, the law says the board can't "ration health care." The board also can't raise taxes or Medicare premiums, make seniors share more of the cost of their benefits, trim the benefits, or change the eligibility rules.

And because hospitals groups were powerful supporters of the legislation—and the Obama administration and Congress wanted to make sure they stayed that way—hospitals can't get hit with any of the cuts until after 2019. Hospices will be exempt until then, too. What that leaves isn't exactly clear—other than, perhaps, proposing even more payment cuts to providers who aren't hospitals.

And it's not clear that Congress will even allow the board to survive. A group of Senate Republicans, led by John Cornyn of Texas, have already introduced legislation to abolish it—the "Health Care Bureaucrats Elimination Act." Republicans aren't likely to get anywhere with their promises to repeal the entire health care law, but they could have more luck knocking out some of the least popular parts of it. And a board of experts that's supposed to cut Medicare could easily become one of the least popular parts of all.

Fears That Budgeting Will Lead to Rationing

Ultimately, budget experts don't believe piecemeal changes will slow Medicare spending enough to make the program affordable. As long as Medicare remains an open-ended program, with no overall limit on what it can spend, they don't believe the costs will ever get under control.

As a result, some of those experts are talking about more substantial, systematic changes to Medicare—like capping the spending so seniors can no longer expect it to pay for everything.

The idea is to "put Medicare on a budget," said Rudolph Penner, a senior fellow at the Urban Institute who writes frequently about budget issues. And in the United States, he said, the only politically acceptable way to do that would be to turn Medicare into something more like a voucher program.

The most prominent example of this approach is a proposal by Ryan, the Republican congressman from Wisconsin, that would give all seniors a fixed payment to help them buy a private insurance plan. If they wanted more generous coverage, they would be able to pay extra for it, Ryan said. But if they chose a lower-cost plan, they could save their extra money or put it to other uses, like long-term care coverage.

The payments would start at $11,000 a year, on average, and they'd be indexed at a rate greater than inflation—but lower than the current rise in medical costs. The amount would be higher for seniors with health problems, and low-income seniors would get more as well. The plan would be phased in, so it would apply only to people who are currently under age 55.

Ryan says his plan is the best way to save the Medicare program from exploding debt and, eventually, from leading to government price controls and direct rationing of care. "There's two ways to go. You can put the government in charge of the system and put down more and more price controls, with sort of 'intelligent rationing' . . . or you can put the doctor and the patient at the nucleus," Ryan said. Any Medicare rescue plan has to get at the root causes of rising costs, he said, and "the market does that better than any other system."

Seniors groups, however, say the proposal itself would be a form of rationing. And liberal groups have promised to fight the proposal, saying it would push seniors into the least efficient kind of health insurance: the individual market, which is full of coverage gaps and unstable premiums. "You'd be throwing one of the most vulnerable populations into the mix of an unscrupulous private health insurance market," said Alex Lawson, communications director for Strengthen Social Security, a coalition of liberal groups that also monitors health care issues.

To get any traction for such a restructuring of Medicare, Republicans would need some support from Democrats, or at least a cease-fire, to protect them from a backlash from seniors. But given how hard Republicans are fighting to either repeal or withhold funding from the Democrats' signature achievement—the health care law—they're not likely to find any goodwill to advance their own proposals.

> "We cannot create a credible road map to a higher-quality, lower-cost health system without using Medicare as a catalyst for widespread private sector reforms."

Reforming Medicare Can Help Lower Health Care Costs

Len M. Nichols

In the following viewpoint, Len M. Nichols asserts that Medicare reforms will provide the catalyst to spark savings throughout the health care system. Nichols advocates the creation of a new Medicare decision-making body that will be immune to lobbying interests and congressional micromanaging and thus be able to draft reforms focused on value and efficiency. To Nichols this will also entail a revamping of the purchasing structure of Medicare so that the suppliers and providers will be encouraged to compete for Medicare dollars. Once this system proves its worth, Nichols believes this high-quality, low-cost model will lead to a reform of the entire health care sector. Len M. Nichols is the director of the Health Policy Program at the New America Foundation, a non-profit public policy institute devoted to ensuring that future generations enjoy better lives.

Len M. Nichols, "Using Medicare to Lower Health Care Costs," *Washington Times*, April 19, 2009. Used by permission of the author.

As you read, consider the following questions:
1. What percent of health care spending does not make patients healthier, as Nichols argues?
2. How does Nichols see information technologies assisting in the lowering of health care spending?
3. Who does Nichols say should delegate specific Medicare decisions to the proposed entity that will carry out value- and evidence-based judgments concerning Medicare spending?

O ur nation must re-establish fiscal balance as soon as macro-economically permissible. At this moment, there is no question that we must take substantive steps to stimulate our economy and address the crises in our housing and financial markets.

In fact, I have never seen such consensus in a profession as argumentative as economics. But America's economic and social futures are also threatened by several long-term challenges. First among these is the ever-rising cost of health care.

Fixing Health Care Entails Fixing Medicare

Health care costs are the largest threat to our nation's fiscal future because Medicare, which accounts for 20 percent of government spending, buys health care from the same inefficient health care system as the rest of us. With Medicare and system-wide health care costs rising faster than economy-wide productivity year after year, the lines between fiscal reform and health reform are increasingly blurred.

Therefore, we should start thinking of health, Medicare and fiscal reforms as inexorably linked. The only way we are going to improve our nation's long-term economic outlook is to fix our health care system.

One way to move toward a more sustainable health system is by using Medicare—the nation's largest purchaser of health

Emphasizing Outcomes Encourages Best Practices

Purchasers care about the health and well-being of patients during and following treatment, and the cost of purchasing such treatment. The clinical choices made by providers (and consumers) are means to those ends; they involve numerous options and reasons for choosing a particular course of action. Improving outcomes may require some providers to choose different clinical processes, or to administer them more consistently. Emphasizing outcomes under VBP [value-based purchasing] would constitute an "open-book test" for providers, who would be motivated to examine their outcomes and their own practices in light of evidence-based or emerging clinical technologies.

Christopher P. Tompkins, Aparna R. Higgins, and Grant A. Ritter, "Measuring Outcomes and Efficiency in Medicare Value-Based Purchasing," Health Affairs, *March/ April 2009. www.healthaffairs.org.*

care—as a catalyst for improving quality, value and efficiency throughout the health care marketplace. Today's Medicare payment structure rewards providers for delivering volume, not value, and for doing more care, not better care. These incentives are perverse. In short, Medicare must buy smarter.

What does buying smarter really mean? Respected analysts estimate that more than 30 percent of what we spend on health care does not make patients healthier. We must reduce this misdirected spending. Medicare could achieve savings and improve patient care by basing its purchasing decisions on value, clinical evidence and observed outcomes.

In the Medicare program, this could mean a payment structure that rewards team-based care and/or new and innovative treatment processes for individuals with chronic diseases. This also means giving doctors and patients more information about what treatments work best and bringing 21st-century technology to health care through electronic medical records and decision-support tools.

Whatever the specific reforms, Medicare and its beneficiaries must get more clinical value for the money they spend on health care. This will improve care for Medicare patients, while lessening the financial burden for taxpayers in the long run.

Yet, Medicare's governance structure hinders its ability to become a value-based purchaser and in doing so perpetuates the health care cost growth problems that threaten our nation's fiscal future. This a result of too much micromanaging by congressional committees and not enough decision-making in the field, as some members of Congress will admit.

Establishing a New Entity to Oversee Medicare Spending

Therefore, we must change the way Medicare is governed to achieve our goals.

This is why I believe (along with several lawmakers and stakeholder organizations) that we should create a new entity to insulate Congress and the White House from lobbying about technical, scientific issues related to the Medicare program. Congress should delegate a set of Medicare decisions to this politically shielded authority, which will then be free to structure value-based payment incentives and make more decisions based on evidence and fewer choices because of politics.

Yet, tackling Medicare reform alone will not solve our problems. We must also improve the efficiency of the entire health care system from which Medicare buys. By revamping Medicare's pricing structure, however, we can create incentives for providers to adopt high-value care processes.

In turn, this should make the delivery of care to the under-65 population more efficient (as did the move to diagnosis-related group payments to hospitals in the 1980s) and inspire private insurers to adopt similar, if not identical, incentive-based contracts. Therefore, we must reform our Medicare program to both improve the budgetary outlook for our nation and incent the delivery system to produce higher-value care at lower costs than it does today.

Medicare Reforms Are the Key

Medicare reform and broader health system reform are inextricably linked to each other and to our nation's fiscal future. We cannot change our Medicare cost trajectories without reforming the broader health system. We cannot create a credible road map to a higher-quality, lower-cost health system without using Medicare as a catalyst for widespread private sector reforms.

We cannot get our fiscal house back in order without slowing the rate of Medicare and health care system cost growth. The goals of comprehensive health reform, Medicare reform and fiscal responsibility should not be viewed separately, but rather jointly.

Our current economic crisis has highlighted the need to finally address our nation's long-term challenges. Meaningful reforms to our Medicare program and our health system are the keys to a more fiscally sustainable economic future.

Periodical Bibliography

The following articles have been selected to supplement the diverse views presented in this chapter.

Scott W. Atlas — "The Worst Study Ever," *Commentary*, April 2011.

Stephen Bezruchka — "Health Equity in the USA," *Social Alternatives*, vol. 29, no. 2, 2010.

Richard Browdie — "The Future of Aging Services in America," *Generations*, Fall 2010.

Richard A. Cooper — "States with More Health Care Spending Have Better-Quality Health Care: Lessons About Medicare," *Health Affairs*, January/February 2009.

David A. Hyman — "Follow the Money: Money Matters in Care, Just Like in Everything Else," *American Journal of Law and Medicine*, vol. 36, no. 2–3, 2010.

Floyd Norris — "The Divided States of Health Care," *New York Times*, October 10, 2009.

Pat Regnier — "Focus on Real Health-Care Risks," *Money*, October 2009.

Robert J. Samuelson — "Let Them Go Bankrupt, Soon," *Newsweek*, June 1, 2009.

Karen Tumulty, Kate Pickert, and Alice Park — "America, the Doctor Will See You Now," *Time*, April 5, 2010.

Grace-Marie Turner and Joseph R. Antos — "Medicare Is No Model for Health Reform," *Wall Street Journal*, September 11, 2009.

Chapter 2

Who Is to Blame for Rising Health Care Costs?

Chapter Preface

Much of the debate about health care focuses on the rapidly growing costs that individuals and families pay for plans and services. Perhaps less attention has been paid to the employer who incurs a sizable burden in health care costs as well. According to certain studies, the burden continues to get heavier every year.

PricewaterhouseCoopers conducted a survey in 2011 of over 1,700 companies in thirty different industries. The assessors found that employer health plans had risen in cost by 7.5 percent in 2010 and 8 percent in 2011 from previous years; they are expected to rise again in 2012. Medical costs are expected to continue an upward trend as health care providers merge, reducing the competition that drives down prices. Medicare and Medicaid increases are also adding to the bill. "Employers continue to be concerned about the sustainability of healthcare cost increases, especially in the long-term, and they are reacting by making changes now," states Michael Thompson, a principal in the human resource services department of Pricewaterhouse-Coopers.

To defray these costs, some employers are looking to purchase high-deductible plans for their workforce. They may also benefit from the reduction of prices of certain drugs that lose their patents and open the door to competitive generic imitators. Much of the answer to the quest for cost reduction, though, might rest on the shoulders of the employees, specifically in their attempts to achieve wellness. As health care costs continue to rise, employers are hoping their workers will adopt healthier lifestyles. In its 2011 Health Care Survey of 1,028 employers surveyed nationwide, the consulting firm Aon Hewitt discovered that employers would like to see costs reduced by: "improving employee health habits (56%), lowering the health care cost trend (49%), decreasing worker health risk (44%), increasing participant awareness of health issues (37%) and enhancing participation in health improvement/disease management programs (37%)."

Employee wellness has even spawned a cottage industry filled with consultants who work one-on-one with companies by implementing health initiatives to improve employee efficiency and cut costs. Some of these offerings include health risk appraisals, health coaching, incentive-based wellness programs, and more. According to the consulting firms involved, the results seem to make a difference. The consulting firm Infinite Health Coach boasts significant return on investment (ROI) figures due to many of their wellness programs. In fact, health risk assessments for Union Pacific and for Johnson & Johnson have yielded $3.6 million and $13 million annual ROI respectively. In their white paper titled *ROI-based Analysis of Employee Wellness Programs*, US Corporate Wellness Inc. finds that a company's commitment to wellness programs can lead to a "20%–55% reduction in health care costs . . . and a drop in work comp and disability by as much as 30%."

The US Centers for Disease Control and Prevention also supports the promotion of wellness in the workplace. They found that for every dollar employers spend on wellness programs, they save $3 to $6 in health care costs. While employers' emphasis on wellness might be profit-driven, it is still beneficial to employees. Each year, the average American faces more diseases related to smoking and obesity than the average European. By improving their health through work-based programs, Americans increase the chances of improving their lives in general.

The success of this model assumes that consumers are part of the solution to cutting health care costs. The authors in the following chapter examine other potential causes for rising health care costs and debate the ways these costs might be mitigated.

> "When asked what they believe to be
> the key drivers of health-care costs,
> U.S. business leaders pointed to . . .
> pharmaceuticals."

Drug Companies Are to Blame for Rising Health Care Costs

PR Newswire

In the following viewpoint, PR Newswire reports on the results of a survey linking prescription drugs and rising health care costs. The majority of US business leaders believe that drug company operations and profit margins are the key drivers of health care cost increases. Health care affordability is being stretched to its limits, and the demand for pharmaceuticals and treatments is impacting the consumer greatly.

As you read, consider the following questions:

1. How much has the average costs of prescriptions risen?
2. What percentage of the health care purchasers surveyed believe prescription drugs are the reason for increasing health care costs?
3. How many Americans may lack health care services?

"Prescription Drug Costs Identified as Main Driver of Increasing U.S. Health-Care Costs," *PR Newswire*, April 24, 2002. Used by permission.

While results from a new Blue Cross and Blue Shield Association [BCBSA] survey reveal that prescription drug costs are the main driver of increasing U.S. health-care costs, Regence BlueShield of Idaho is working to keep its members' costs low.

The statewide company has been a leader in controlling prescription costs for its members. While the national average of cost per member per month of prescriptions has risen between 17 and 22 percent each year since 1999, Regence BlueShield of Idaho has kept its growth rate in the low teens. This has been accomplished by focused education of physicians regarding drug costs and broad education of members on how to utilize their prescription benefit to control their own, as well as overall, prescription costs.

Informed Health-Care Consumers

Terry Killilea, assistant vice president of Pharmacy Services for Regence BlueShield of Idaho, said it's important that consumers get involved in working with their health-care provider to keep costs low.

"We encourage our members to be informed health-care consumers, to get involved in their health, and to become an active partner in helping to control health-care costs," Killilea said. "By being an informed consumer, you help control these rising costs."

Killilea said there are many ways to become an informed consumer, one of which is simply asking your physician about prescription drugs and the options that are available.

"You can work with your physician to greatly reduce your prescription copayments," Killilea said. "You can often lower your prescription drug costs by asking your doctor for a lower cost generic or a brand on the preferred drug list." . . .

Survey Results

The recent association survey said that 64 percent of health-care benefits purchasers cite prescription drugs as the leading rea-

Drug Companies Raise Prices Prior to Coming Health Care Reform

Wholesale Drug Price

Inflation −1.3*

+8.7%*

Wholesale Price Increases in the Last Year

	Use	Drug Maker	'09 Daily Cost	12-Month Increase*
Boniva (150mg)	osteoporosis	Roche	$2.96	+18.6%
Actos (30mg)	diabetes	Takeda	6.74	+16.5
Singulair (10mg)	asthma	Merck	3.64	+12.5
Enbrel (50mg)	arthritis	Amgen	55.46	+12.1
Plavix (75mg)	anticoagulant	Bristol-Myers Squibb	4.80	+8.2
Nexium (40mg)	ulcer	AstraZeneca	5.16	+7.1
Lipitor (10mg)	cholesterol	Pfizer	2.67	+5.0

*Change over 12 months ending Sept. 30, 2009

TAKEN FROM: Duff Wilson, "Drug Makers Raise Prices in Face of Health Care Reform," *New York Times*, November 16, 2009.

son for increasing health-care costs nationwide. Of that group, 62 percent said that increased direct-to-consumer advertising is the main cause for the continued dramatic rise in pharmaceutical. A total of 44 percent said research and development is a driver of increased pharmaceutical costs while 36 percent said profit margins is the main reason.

More than 500 business decision-makers were asked what they believe are the key drivers behind rapidly accelerating health-care costs. Double-digit health-care cost increases have returned after nearly a decade of slower growth.

"These results are very significant," said Scott P. Serota, president and chief executive officer of the Blue Cross and Blue Shield Association. "The health-care purchasers represented in this survey are on the frontline of America's health-care cost battle. Everyday, they are trying to find ways to keep quality health care affordable for their workers. When asked what they believe to be the key drivers of health-care cost, U.S. business leaders pointed overwhelmingly to pharmaceuticals."

Beyond the impact of pharmaceutical costs, benefits managers said that consumers (33 percent) and hospitals (30 percent) were the next key drivers of health-care cost increases. Reasons given for the consumer impact on costs were the aging of the baby-boomer population, demand for drugs and treatment, as well as growing overall usage of the health-care system. Costs associated with the uninsured, technology advances and facilities expansion were the top considerations given to increased hospital costs.

"Nearly 40 million Americans may lack the health-care services they need because they can't afford health insurance," said Serota. "Rising hospital and pharmaceutical costs, new technology, increased utilization and government regulations are stretching health care affordability to its limits. Add to that the changing demographics of an aging baby-boomer population and the problem, if not addressed, will worsen. The Blue Cross and Blue Shield System is determined to make a difference for today's generation and tomorrow's."

BCBSA and the 43 independently licensed Blue Plans have embarked on a multi-year initiative to reach out to key stakeholders in the U.S. health-care system to find ways to make health care more affordable while maintaining quality and choice. BCBSA is conducting a series of research projects designed to provide valuable information to be used to improve health-care affordability.

> "[President Barack Obama has suggested] that America spends too much on prescription drugs—implying that drug prices are responsible for our high health-care costs. This is a popular misconception."

Drug Companies Are Not to Blame for Rising Health Care Costs

Sally C. Pipes

Sally C. Pipes is president and chief executive officer of the Pacific Research Institute, a San Francisco–based think tank. She writes a regular column for Investor's Business Daily *and her opinion pieces on health care have appeared in major news outlets such as the* Wall Street Journal, USA Today, *and the* New York Times. *In the viewpoint that follows, she refutes the notion that drug companies are driving health-care costs. Pipes claims that drugs are cost-effective, preventative therapies that keep most Americans from having to pay for hospital treatment and surgical costs to combat chronic diseases. She also insists that drug prices have been falling in recent years despite arguments to the contrary.*

Sally C. Pipes, "Don't Blame Drugs for Health-Care Costs," *National Review Online,* March 11, 2009. www.nationalreview.com. Used by permission.

As you read, consider the following questions:

1. What accounts for 85 percent of all US health care spending, according to Pipes?
2. According to a paper from the National Bureau of Economic Research, cited by the author, how much money does Medicare save for every dollar spent on medicines?
3. As Pipes reports, how much money do drug companies spend on average to bring a new drug to market?

In the opening pages of his recently released budget [for 2009], Pres. Barack Obama describes the rising cost of health care as "one of the big drains on family budgets and on the performance of the economy as a whole." Later in the budget, he suggests that America spends too much on prescription drugs—implying that drug prices are responsible for our high health-care costs. This is a popular misconception, and it will likely hinder Obama's plan to revamp the U.S. health system.

Drugs Reduce Overall Medical Spending

At first glance, it's understandable that some believe drug expenditures are inflating overall health-care costs. In 2007, the United States spent $286.5 billion on prescription drugs. To put that figure in perspective, it's more than the entire GDP [gross domestic product] of Ireland. In isolation, that's impressive. But one must remember that prescription drugs actually *reduce* medical spending by obviating the need for prolonged hospital stays and expensive surgeries.

Among the biggest drivers of rising health-care spending are chronic diseases. These are illnesses, such as diabetes and heart disease, that demand regular treatment over the course of a patient's life. Between 1994 and 2004, the prevalence of diabetes doubled. High blood pressure is also on the rise. And heart disease now kills one person every 34 seconds.

Caring for people with chronic diseases now accounts for about 85 percent of all U.S. health-care spending. Thus, one of the most effective ways to lower overall health-care costs would be to control chronic diseases. And drugs have proven to be one of the most effective—and least expensive—ways to do that.

A 2005 study published in the journal *Medical Care* found that every additional dollar spent on drugs for blood pressure, cholesterol, and diabetes reduces other health-care spending by an average of $4 to $7. Similarly, a [September 2007] paper from the National Bureau of Economic Research estimated that Medicare saves $2.06 for every dollar it spends on medicines. This makes sense. A daily dosage of Lipitor is cheaper than emergency heart surgery.

The Cost of Drug Development Is Falling

Of course, drugs are not necessarily cheap. The process of developing a new drug is extraordinarily expensive—on average, it takes 10 to 15 years and $1.3 billion to bring a new drug to market. This tremendous investment is reflected in the prices we pay. In recent years, however, there has been evidence that drug prices are falling.

In September 2007, the U.S. Department of Labor reported that the annual inflation rate for drug prices was at its lowest point in the three decades since Labor began tracking it. The annual inflation rate was 1 percent, well under the rate of overall inflation.

President Obama would be wise to keep this in mind as he moves forward on health-care reform. If he doesn't, he could end up hurting the industry that is most able to drive health-care prices down.

| "In health care, more is not always
better—and it's often worse."

Overprescribed and Dangerous Treatments Contribute to Rising Health Care Costs

Ellen-Marie Whelan and Sonia Sekhar

In the following viewpoint, Ellen-Marie Whelan and Sonia Sekhar assert that wasteful and inefficient medical treatments contribute to rising health care costs. Whelan and Sekhar argue that many practices and prescriptions—including x-rays, surgeries, and antibiotics—are overprescribed and often have little or no effect on the health outcomes of patients. More worrisome, the authors believe some unnecessary treatments have proven dangerous to patients' health. The authors claim that doctors tend to overprescribe treatments for a variety of reasons, including paid reimbursement and ignorance of best practices. Whelan and Sekhar advocate health care reform that reins in this waste by reimbursing doctors based on quality of health outcomes instead of quantity of tests and treatments. Ellen-Marie Whelan is a senior health policy analyst and associate director of health policy at the Center for American Progress, a progressive public policy research institute. Sonia Sekhar is a former research assistant with the Center for American Progress.

Ellen-Marie Whelan and Sonia Sekhar, "Costly and Dangerous Treatments Weigh Down Health Care," Center for American Progress, July 9, 2009. Used by permission.

As you read, consider the following questions:

1. According to the authors' research, what percent of medical imaging may be unnecessary because the results do not help patient health outcomes?
2. As Whelan and Sekhar report, how much do Americans spend each year on inappropriate antibiotic treatments for colds and flu?
3. In what way do Whelan and Sekhar advocate reforming health information technologies to help lower health care costs?

Our health care system is wrought with inefficiencies and waste that account for up to $700 billion of health care spending annually. Indeed, some researchers speculate that one-third or more of all treatments and procedures performed in the United States have no proven benefits. What's more, a number of these unhelpful services produce hazardous side effects in patients. All too often, by the time studies are performed to determine these health services' effectiveness, the nation has spent millions, or in some cases billions, of dollars on them. It is crucial to reduce the unnecessary costs that are dragging down our health system's efficiency. Recognizing and eliminating the utilization of unnecessary services can increase savings in the system, help slow the staggering growth rate of health care costs, and keep our population healthier.

The overuse of health services is in part due to the lack of comparative effectiveness research—research that tells us what works and what doesn't, especially when comparing two different treatments for the same illness. Most research done today only examines whether a certain service works compared to doing nothing—but doesn't indicate which works best among a range of possibilities. Comparative effectiveness research sometimes compares similar treatments, such as competing drugs, or a brand new drug versus a known generic. Or the research may compare very different therapies such as major surgery compared to just taking a medication.

But the provision of unnecessary services is not entirely due to lack of information; some services are overused or overprovided because of perverse financial incentives. Our current medical reimbursement system pays much more generously for high-tech, high-cost services while underpaying for primary care, prevention, and chronic illness management. We reimburse health care providers based on volume: more tests, more services, [and] more money. This can be more expensive and dangerous.

Unnecessary Services Are Inappropriate and Potentially Dangerous

We are fortunate to benefit from dramatic new advances in medicine that have undoubtedly saved and improved countless lives. But the new advancements do not always provide better care for everyone. Some of the reliable older treatment might still be the best choice for some patients.

Heart stents, for example, have saved numerous lives since their introduction, yet evidence now indicates that stents are being overused with some dangerous outcomes. The procedure for placing a stent is quite invasive: It requires an angioplasty, can be painful, and is not without side effects. A study published in the *New England Journal of Medicine* [*NEJM*] found that it is less expensive and just as effective to treat many heart attack patients with drugs instead of angioplasty with stent. Researchers found that the stents were unnecessary in many cases and that those receiving the drug treatment only had a slightly longer life expectancy. Other studies found the overuse of unnecessary stents is leading to thousands of heart attacks and deaths each year. Unnecessary use of heart stents is also expensive—providing unnecessary stents to the 100,000 heart attack patients in the United States that do not need them costs $700 million a year.

Researchers estimate that the cost of overuse of spinal surgery for low back pain is even more expensive than stents, and exceeds $11 billion each year. Another study estimates that 70 percent of the women receiving a hysterectomy did not need this major abdominal surgery and would have benefited from less severe therapies. In this case nearly 450,000 women undergo an unnecessary surgery, which requires weeks of recovery, at the cost of an additional $1.1 billion each year.

Unnecessary Services Are Ineffective and Overused

Researchers are finding that many procedures may be a waste of time and money. We know it's better—and cheaper—to get the treatment right the first time and no one wants to waste time getting a treatment that hasn't been shown to work. But that doesn't always happen.

One prime example is radiology services. Recent studies show that 20 percent to 50 percent of medical imaging—a $100 billion-a-year industry including CT, MRI, and PET scans—is unnecessary because the results do not help diagnose ailments or treat patients. It is generally not dangerous to get an extra X-ray, but researchers believe that the radiation from CT studies may account for between 1.5 percent and 2 percent of cancer cases in the United States. The most striking thing about the overuse of radiologic imaging is the cost. Economists estimate that this overuse accounts for between $18 billion and $33 billion of overall health care spending.

Another very expensive and systemic problem with the health system occurs when patients have to be re-hospitalized because of care they did or did not receive while in the hospital or when they were discharged. The *New England Journal of Medicine* [*NEJM*] just reported that almost one fifth (19.6 percent) of Medicare beneficiaries were re-hospitalized within 30 days of being discharged, and another 34 percent were re-hospitalized within 90 days. Over half of the patients never saw a doctor in the month after discharge. The extra hospitalization is both an inconvenience for patients and potentially a safety hazard. And it is very expensive for the Medicare program and the nation. The authors of that same study estimated that unplanned re-hospitalizations cost Medicare $17.4 billion in 2004.

Taking antibiotics for a common cold is another overused service that has no benefit to the patient. Antibiotics kill bacteria and are therefore completely ineffective in treating viral upper respiratory infections such as cold and flu. This treatment also costs the nation nearly $550 million every year. And excessive use of antibiotics has contributed to the emergence and spread of antibiotic-resistant bacteria in many communities.

We Can Promote Better Care at Lower Costs

In health care, more is not always better—and it's often worse. Who wants to have an unnecessary surgery? Who wants to take medicine that doesn't work? What these and the following examples suggest is that more medical care may actually be contributing to poorer health outcomes.

We must first learn what works and what does not in order to address the problem of unnecessary services. As Dr. Atul Gwande noted in the *New Yorker* and researchers have documented, there is less variation in services when the right treatment is well established. But all too often we just do not know what works best. Comparative effectiveness research will help provide guidance about which treatments, drugs, and devices work best for a given condition.

We also need to change the payment system so that it compensates health providers based on quality rather than quantity. Today we get what we pay for. We pay for high-tech, high-volume services and we get a fragmented system of health care focused on specialty care rather than primary care. We need to move payment away from rewarding more tests and procedures and toward reimbursing primary care, care coordination, and prevention.

In order to measure better outcomes we will also need to invest in better health information technologies [IT] to help medical practices monitor patients and to keep track of how they are doing. Health IT systems should be designed in conjunction with payment reform policies. Health IT, if properly developed, has the potential to offer the health care team critical support in providing comprehensive preventive care, chronic-care disease management, improved care coordination across providers, and patient education.

Researchers at Dartmouth University have found that the areas of the country with the highest costs and highest volume of services have the poorest health outcomes. What's more, patients in areas of the country that deliver more expensive, high-tech services report less satisfaction with health care than patients in areas with lower spending. Health care reform provides us with an opportunity to get better care and better value by promoting more and better comparative effectiveness research, providing better financial incentives for health professionals, and encouraging better use of health IT. Our health and financial well-being depend on replacing the overprescription of unnecessary services with support for better care at lower costs.

Inappropriate—and Potentially Hazardous—Procedures

Hysterectomies A study in *Obstetrics and Gynecology* found that the majority of surgeries removing a women's uterus were completely unnecessary.

Health: Up to 70 percent of hysterectomies performed have been judged as inappropriate by experts. This represents nearly 450,000 women who undergo major abdominal surgery and weeks of recovery.

Cost: Unnecessary hysterectomies account for over $1.1 billion of waste in spending.

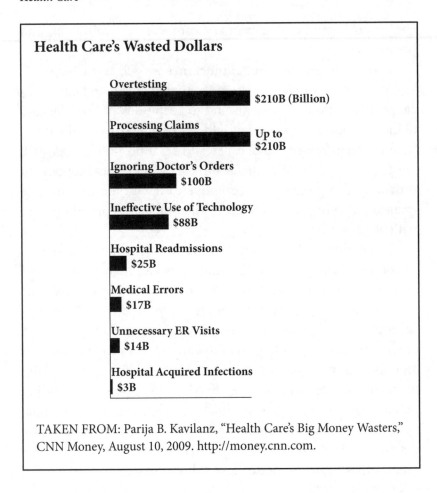

Health Care's Wasted Dollars

Overtesting
$210B (Billion)

Processing Claims
Up to $210B

Ignoring Doctor's Orders
$100B

Ineffective Use of Technology
$88B

Hospital Readmissions
$25B

Medical Errors
$17B

Unnecessary ER Visits
$14B

Hospital Acquired Infections
$3B

TAKEN FROM: Parija B. Kavilanz, "Health Care's Big Money Wasters," CNN Money, August 10, 2009. http://money.cnn.com.

Heart stents Stents have saved countless lives, but evidence now indicates that in many cases stents are being overused with some dangerous outcomes. The procedure for placing a stent involves an angioplasty, is invasive, painful, and not without side effects. To place a stent, a catheter is routed up a large blood vessel in the groin and the wire stent is inserted and expands an artery.

A *NEJM* study in 2006 found that it is less expensive and just as effective to treat many heart attack patients with drugs instead of angioplasty with stent.

Health: Not only did the researchers find that the angioplasty with stent was unnecessary in many cases, they also found slightly longer life expectancy for those with the drug treatment only.

Cost: The same authors calculated the costs associated with drug therapy compared to the unnecessary stenting. They estimated that 100,000 heart attack patients in the United States do not need stents, and this could translate to annual savings of $700 million.

A January 2009 study published in *NEJM* shows that stents have been overused in situations where a simple blood-flow test could prevent unnecessary and potentially dangerous care.

Health: Researchers speculate that the use of stents when they are not necessary is leading to thousands of heart attacks and deaths each year.

A 2007 *NEJM* study compared the effects of two treatments: an angioplasty with a metal stent combined with a drug regimen versus the drug regimen alone.

Health: The study found that patients treated with angioplasty and a stent had better blood flow and fewer symptoms of heart problems initially, but the differences declined over time. More importantly, it found no differences between the two groups in survival rates or the occurrence of heart attacks over a five-year period.

Spinal-fusion surgery A February 2004 analysis of spinal-fusion surgery published in *NEJM* concluded that its efficacy for the most common indications remains unclear.

Health: This type of back surgery leads to more complications than other types of spinal surgery.

Cost: Inappropriate spinal-fusion surgeries account for approximately $11.1 billion of waste in health care spending a year. There were over 303,000 spinal-fusion surgeries in 2004, and the average hospital bill is over $34,000, not including professional fees. What's more, the amount Medicare spends on fusion surgeries has risen 500 percent over a decade and now represents nearly half of the $1 billion that Medicare spends on all spine surgeries.

Lung surgery The *NEJM* reported on a trial in 2003 that compared the effects of lung volume surgery with standard medical therapy (medicines, oxygen, and pulmonary rehabilitation) for patients suffering from emphysema. This surgery had anecdotal support but lacked hard evidence about its effectiveness.

Health: Lung surgery increased many patients' risk of death slightly and did not improve their functional status.

Antihypertensive drugs A landmark eight-year study published in the *Journal of the American Medical Association* in 2002 found "that relatively inexpensive blood-pressure-lowering drugs, known as diuretics, worked better than newer, more expensive calcium channel blockers and ACE inhibitors."

Health: During the course of the study the researchers had to stop comparing one of the newer drugs since it caused substantially more cardiovascular problems, especially hospitalizations for heart failure, compared to the others.

Cost: Older diuretic drug use declined from 56 percent to 27 percent of antihypertensive prescriptions between 1982 and 1992. If the treatment remained at the 1982 level, the health care system would have saved $3.1 billion over those 10 years.

Arthroscopic surgery for osteoarthritis *NEJM* published a study of a trial in 2008 that compared arthroscopic knee surgery for osteoarthritis patients with physical therapy and medication.

Health: The researchers found that arthroscopic surgery for these patients provides no additional benefit compared to traditional medical care. Knee surgery was in fact an unnecessary surgery that did not help these patients.

Cost: The nation spends over $2 billion annually on arthroscopic knee surgery for people with osteoarthritis—a surgery we now know does not help these individuals.

Overused Services and Procedures

Use of antibiotics for the common cold Antibiotics kill bacteria and are therefore completely ineffective in treating viral upper respiratory infections (cold and flu). Using these unnecessary drugs costs the nation nearly $550 million annually.

Overuse: The Commonwealth Fund's National Scorecard on U.S. Health System Performance finds that 35 percent of children with a sore throat are potentially inappropriately prescribed antibiotics. Each year in the United States, an estimated 50 million antibiotic prescriptions are for illnesses such as colds or flu for which antibiotics offer no benefit.

Health: The excessive use of antibiotics has contributed to the emergence and spread of antibiotic-resistant bacteria in many communities. Antibiotic resistance is causing fewer drugs to be effective to treat many infectious diseases. The remaining alternative drugs may be less effective, more expensive, and more difficult to administer.

Cost: The unnecessary use of antibiotics accounts for up to $550 million in wasted spending each year. In addition, the rise in antibiotic-resistant bacteria demands the development of new kinds of treatments for superbugs.

Prostate cancer screening A recent study in *NEJM* on the effectiveness of prostate cancer screening versus a prostate-specific antigen (PSA, a blood test) showed that the rate of death from prostate cancer was very low and did not differ significantly between the group that received an annual PSA test and the group that received usual care.

Overuse: Only 25 percent of men who had a positive PSA test turned out to have prostate cancer. This means that three out of four of the men who had positive tests were "false" positives.

Health: Men who had false-positive results had to go through intensive follow-up procedures, including invasive biopsies, which have their own side effects.

Cost: In addition to the cost of the initial screening, there are the additional costs from the follow-up screenings.

Medical imaging Recent studies show that 20 percent to 50 percent of medical imaging—a $100 billion-a-year industry including CT, MRI, and PET scans—are unnecessary because their results do not help diagnose ailments or treat patients.

Overuse: Diagnostic imaging services delivered in Medicare grew more rapidly than any other type of physician service between 1999 and 2003. Physician services grew on average 22 percent in those years, but imaging services grew by 45 percent—twice as fast. Some specific services grew even faster: MRIs grew by 99 percent, and CT scans grew 82 percent. The Commonwealth Fund also found about one quarter of imaging services for lower-back pain were potentially inappropriate. The National Scorecard on U.S. Health System Performance finds that 26 percent of adult private health plan members and 22 percent of Medicaid recipients received an unnecessary imaging study within the month following an acute low back pain episode.

Health: Radiation from CT studies may account for between 1.5 percent and 2 percent of cancer cases in the United States.

Cost: Overuse of noninvasive radiologic imaging accounts for between $18.2 billion and $33.3 billion in overall health care spending waste. Even the private sector concurs. A group of medical insurers led by WellPoint and Magellan Health Services claim that medical scans waste $30 billion a year (specifically noted are MRIs and CT scans). Indeed, Medicare spending for imaging services grew over 60 percent in only four years from $5.7 billion in 1999 to $9.3 billion in 2003.

Preventable unnecessary hospital readmissions NEJM just this year [2009] reported that almost one-fifth (19.6 percent) of Medicare beneficiaries who had been discharged from a hospital were re-hospitalized within 30 days, and another 34.0 percent were re-hospitalized within 90 days. Over half of the patients *never* saw a doctor in the month after discharge.

Cost: Unplanned re-hospitalizations cost Medicare $17.4 billion in 2004.

> *"It may be Americans' own habits that are driving health care costs in the United States."*

Consumer Behavior Contributes to Rising Health Care Costs

Raja Jagadeesan

Raja Jagadeesan is a medical doctor and a member of the ABC News Medical Unit that reports on health affairs. In the following viewpoint, Jagadeesan cites studies that blame US health care costs partly on the bad behaviors and unhealthy vices of Americans. Jagadeesan reports how smoking and lack of exercise have made Americans less healthy than Europeans, forcing the nation to spend more per person on health care. Jagadeesan asserts that Americans could save more money on medical bills if they just took better care of their health.

As you read, consider the following questions:

1. About how much does the average American spend annually on health care, as Jagadeesan reports?
2. According to research cited by the author, what percent of Americans are overweight? And what percent of

Raja Jagadeesan, "Preventable Illness at Core of US Health Costs," ABC News Medical Unit, October 3, 2007. Used by permission of ABCNews.com.

Europeans are overweight?

3. As Jagadeesan states, approximately how much could Americans save each year on health care costs if they could reduce the prevalence of chronic disease to European levels?

John Smith, from a health care perspective, is a typical American.

He is a 56-year-old white male living in a suburban city in the United States. He has been an on-again, off-again smoker throughout his life but recently quit—something he is proud of.

He is 5 feet 9 inches tall and weighs 190 pounds, and he knows he could probably stand to lose a few pounds. Scientists would calculate his body mass index at 28, a classification that qualifies him as overweight.

As John Smith prepares for retirement, he also realizes that 18 percent of his income goes toward health care costs, and he wonders why he is paying so much.

John Smith is not real. But he does represent the type of average American over age 50 examined in a study published this week by researchers at Emory University's School of Public Health.

And according to the study, it may be Americans' own habits that are driving health care costs in the United States.

The average American spends more than $6,000 each year on health care—the highest amount in the world and twice as much as Europeans spend. In the past, the most common reasons cited for this difference were increased access to medical providers, higher use of advanced technologies, and higher prices for services.

However, the study in this week's [October 2007] issue of the journal *Health Affairs* suggests that Americans' obesity and smoking habits may be partly to blame, and may be costing Americans $100 billion to $150 billion per year.

Chronic Ills Mean Costly Care

Researchers examined the rates of 10 of the most common and costly chronic illnesses among those over age 50. The illnesses included diabetes, hypertension, arthritis, heart disease, high cholesterol, chronic lung disease, asthma, osteoporosis, stroke and cancer.

Overall, the rates were significantly higher in the United States than in Europe. In most cases, Americans were also more likely to receive medications for the same medical diagnosis.

The researchers also looked for potential reasons to explain why Americans have higher rates of disease than Europeans. One glaring finding from the study was that obesity and smoking were more prevalent in the United States.

Thirty-three percent of Americans were obese, compared with only 17 percent of Europeans. In addition, 53 percent of Americans had smoked at some point in their lives, compared with 43 percent of Europeans.

In addition, every chronic illness closely linked to obesity or smoking was more common in the United States.

Lead study author Kenneth Thorpe, a professor of health policy at Emory's Rollins School of Public Health and former deputy assistant secretary of Health and Human Services, said that some of the findings were surprising.

"We had some idea of what we would find," said Thorpe. "We knew that obesity and smoking rates would be higher in the U.S. But the extent of the differences, especially with some of the chronic illnesses such as hypertension, heart disease and diabetes, was higher than we anticipated."

According to the study, Americans were more than 50 percent more likely to have high blood pressure or diabetes, almost twice as likely to have heart disease, and 2½ times more likely to have arthritis.

This added burden of disease has led to higher health costs overall. If the United States could improve its population's health to have the same levels of chronic illness as Europeans do,

Americans would save between $1,200 and $1,750 per year each on medical bills, the researchers found.

All told, the higher rates of disease are costing Americans between $100 billion and $150 billion per year, or 13 percent to 19 percent of total health care spending for those age 50 and over.

According to Thorpe, these findings could have a significant impact on strategies to control health care costs in America.

"If you are going to craft effective interventions," said Thorpe, "you have to understand where we are spending the money and what is driving costs over time."

Become Healthy and Save Money

The good news, Thorpe said, is that many of the differences in the study are likely due to reversible causes—causes Americans have control over. "The underpinnings of our findings deal with modifiable factors such as weight, exercise and smoking."

Some experts believe that the relatively poor performance by Americans may become an instigator for personal change.

"What's new is that other people like us are healthier," said Dr. David Katz, associate professor of public health at Yale University. "Europeans are doing better, and we are doing worse. This relatively bad performance might be a motivator."

Others, however, say the findings show that large-scale changes are needed. "A normal weight and healthy lifestyle is very clearly a huge health benefit, especially regarding chronic diseases," said Keith Ayoob, associate professor of pediatrics at Albert Einstein College of Medicine. "There needs to be a national call to action to address prevention and treatment of obesity and cessation of smoking."

Dr. George Blackburn, associate professor of nutrition at Harvard Medical School, had a much more targeted message to the readers of Thorpe's study.

"Figure out a motivator to eat less, eat healthy and exercise," he said. "We could save a lot of money if we had a healthier lifestyle. It would be more fun, and it would feel and taste good."

Periodical Bibliography

The following articles have been selected to supplement the diverse views presented in this chapter.

Michelle Andrews	"Get a Grip on Rising Health Care Costs," *Money*, November 2010.
Geoff Colvin	"'We All Pay for the Uninsured,'" *Fortune*, May 12, 2008.
Economist	"Life Should Be Cheap," January 21, 2011.
Laura D. Hermer and Howard Brody	"Defensive Medicine, Cost Containment, and Reform," *JGIM: Journal of General Internal Medicine*, May 2010.
Avery Johnson	"Race to Pin Blame for Health Costs," *Wall Street Journal*, February 26, 2010.
Jonathan Kellerman	"The Health Insurance Mafia," *Wall Street Journal*, April 14, 2008.
David Kendall	"Health Care Costs and Malpractice Reform," *American Interest*, January–February 2008.
New American	"Reforming Health Insurance," May 10, 2010.
Kate Pickert	"Malpractice Reform," *Time*, September 28, 2009.
Marilyn Werber Sarafini	"Less Competition, Higher Premiums," *National Journal*, March 20, 2010.

CHAPTER 3

How Should Health Care Be Reformed?

Chapter Preface

Defining the government's role in health care continues to challenge pundits, politicians, health care professionals, and citizens alike. For some, health care is a human right; therefore, government should do what it can to sustain an affordable, efficient system for its people. For others, health care is a service, provided by the private sector. Government, to these advocates, has no role in this marketplace other than to provide an opportunity for competition to thrive. Identifying the place of government in health care is among the most heated issues facing the country today.

According to Health Pac, a universal health care advocacy group, "The solution to our health care crisis is in developing a new system of health insurance—one that is more focused on providing equitable access rather than making a profit for big business." Health Pac believes the nation needs single-payer health insurance coverage with the government funding a non-profit system through taxation or mandating the purchase of health care by all citizens who can afford it. While critics deem this socialized medicine, Health Pac contends that the United States participates in this type of system already. Medical departments in the military, veterans hospitals, Medicare, and Medicaid are all types of government-involved health care. Health Pac advocates extending such services to every American in order to create universal care.

The single-payer system, which groups all citizens into a single insurance pool that is managed by the government, defines only how health care is financed, not necessarily how services are provided. For example, the government might pay for some (or even all) of one's health care expenses, but the services themselves would likely be rendered by nongovernmental hospitals and doctors who would collect the fees. This model is essentially the one already adopted by Medicare and Medicaid.

To insure everyone, however, would require a large public fund maintained through taxation, but no one is certain of how the funds appropriated through taxation would compare to the costs of current private-insurer health plans. Although some defenders of the single-payer system argue that the price tag would go down because government management would reduce administrative costs, critics claim the unchecked availability of services would encourage more people to use the system more often—even when medical care may not be needed—and thus raise the overall costs.

Staunch opponents of universal health care frown upon the potential costs, but their argument goes beyond this concern, insisting that health care is not within the purview of government. Conservatives and libertarians represent the strongest voices in opposition. Traditionally these political factions insist upon limited government, personal responsibility, and free markets—all of which are incompatible with universal health care. Their solutions to rising health care costs include minimizing superfluous lawsuits and promoting more competition among insurers. In its website's "statement of purpose" on health care, the Leadership for America Campaign of the Heritage Foundation, a conservative public policy think tank, maintains, "Health plans and providers should be forced to compete on a level playing field in a free and open market where government will not be in the business of picking winners and losers." Such a path to reform emphasizes consumer choice while rejecting government mandates.

Most Americans agree that the current health care system is in need of reform, but how reform is defined remains in question. For some, reform entails the implementation of universal coverage, providing services to everyone, particularly those who cannot afford it. Others conceive of appropriate reform as engendering free-market competition in an effort to moderate costs and, in turn, prevent higher taxes. Regardless of such choices, identifying the role that the government should play in the health care system is crucial in determining how to fix it. The authors in the following chapter debate these alternatives and the place of government in health care. Though each offers different solutions, most agree that the system left as it is will never effectively address the growing health concerns of American citizens.

> "Universal access to health care is the
> practical road to health care reform
> in terms of improved quality and cost
> containment, but more importantly it
> is the right thing to do."

America Needs Universal Health Care

Eric R. Kingson and John M. Cornman

The United States is one of the few developed nations that has not implemented nationalized health care. In the following viewpoint, Eric R. Kingson and John M. Cornman claim that despite some problems associated with universal health care, the United States should adopt a nationalized system. According to the authors, universal care has proven to be less expensive and would likely improve health care access and outcomes for Americans. In addition, Kingson and Cornman maintain that nationalized health care is a logical, moral imperative for a country that values shared responsibility, mutual support, and a vision of government acting in the best interest of citizens. Eric R. Kingson is a professor of social work and public administration at Syracuse University in New York. John M. Cornman is the president and founder of the Alliance of Housing Solutions, a nonprofit organization that advocates for affordable

Eric R. Kingson and John M. Cornman, "Health Care Reform: Universal Access Is Feasible and Necessary," *Benefits Quarterly*, vol. 23, no. 3, Third Quarter 2007, pp. 27–33. Used by permission of the International Society of Certified Employee Benefits Specialists.

housing in Northern Virginia. He has served on the boards of several other nonprofit organizations.

As you read, consider the following questions:

1. According to a *New York Times*/CBS poll cited by the authors, what percent of Americans agreed that the federal government should guarantee health insurance to every American?
2. As Kingson and Cornman report, without reform, what is expected to happen to the total health care expenditures in the United States by 2016?
3. According to what three criteria do Kingson and Cornman believe successful health care reform should be measured?

Health care costs are increasing. Access to health care is declining. The occupationally based health insurance system is greatly stressed; some say "crumbling." Needed public programs, notably Medicare and Medicaid, strain the taxing capacities of government. And, as a share of the nation's gross domestic product (GDP), health care expenditures have increased from 12.4% in 1980 to 16% today and are projected to grow to 20% by 2016.

Almost no one is happy with the current state of affairs. Not employers that see their bottom lines and international competitiveness undermined by health care costs. Not benefit professionals who are called upon to contain the cost of employer plans. Not employees who watch their premiums and copayments increase while the surety and scope of benefits diminish. Not government officials. Not health care providers. Not the public, whose dissatisfaction as measured by EBRI's [Employee Benefit Research Institute's] *2006 Health Confidence Survey* has doubled since 1998—with 59% now rating the system of health care in America poor (31%) or fair (28%) and the remainder as good (25%), very good (5%) or excellent (4%). And certainly not the 47 million Americans who lack health insurance.

Public Interest in Universal Coverage

So, comprehensive reform of the nation's health care "system" is, once again, at the center of the domestic agenda. Interested in expanding access to quality care and constraining cost increases, the general public and many political, business, labor and health care leaders are calling for reform—in some instances forming coalitions that span traditional differences within and between the groups they represent.

"An overwhelming majority," according to a recent *New York Times*/CBS poll, believes "the health care system needs fundamental change or total reorganization." Seventy percent identify the large number of persons without health insurance as a very serious problem for the United States. Sixty-four percent agree that the federal government should guarantee health insurance to every American, especially children. And 60% report that they are willing to pay up to $500 to expand health care coverage for all Americans.

Even so, as in the past, public and opinion leader consensus on how to proceed is limited. In this same *New York Times*/CBS poll, when given a choice between two transforming options, 47% preferred "a national health insurance program covering everyone, administered by the government and financed by tax-payers," and 38% preferred the current financing system.

To forge a stronger consensus, two of the principal concerns of the 38% of Americans who prefer the current funding system must be addressed convincingly—specifically, (1) distrust of large government programs and (2) the twin fears that more government and major changes will automatically mean lower quality health care.

We believe these concerns, while understandable, are not well supported. The experience of other industrial nations shows that universal coverage and more favorable consumer satisfaction is achievable at costs well below health care expenditures in this country. Further, the fear of change is not supported by a considerable body of research showing that containment of health care costs and expenditures does not automatically lower the quality of health care. Neither does a larger government role.

Most centrally, we believe there is a moral imperative, one arising from widely shared social and religious values, to provide universal access to quality care for all members of the national community and that this concern should remain at the core of the new national health care reform discussion. There is no acceptable substitute for universal access as a right of U.S. citizenship. Moreover, as the international experience suggests, universal access and government involvement in assuring such are a necessary prerequisite to controlling health care expenditures and overall cost.

Some Dissatisfaction with National Health Care

Opponents of expanded roles for government in assuring universal access to needed health care—whether through a national health system approach as in the United Kingdom, a single-payer approach as in Canada or a national health insurance approach financed primarily by mandated employer and employee payments as in Germany—often argue that these systems just don't work very well. They charge that the systems are costly and bureaucratic and undermine good medicine, good markets and good sense.

Opponents of single-payer, national health insurance or employer mandate approaches in the U.S. context often point to selected health care problems in other nations to support their assertions that these models are not worthy of consideration in the United States. "If the Canadian system was so good, why would so many Canadians seek high-tech care in the United States?" "The British system of socialized medicine is bureaucratic and many people have to wait a long time for needed treatment." "The Germans have their own health financing crisis."

Not surprisingly, no system is perfect. For example, analyzing data from the *2002 Commonwealth Fund International Health Policy Survey of Sicker Adults in the United States, Canada, the United Kingdom, Australia, and New Zealand,* Robert Blendon, professor of health policy at Harvard's School of Public Health, and his colleagues find that there is widespread dissatisfaction among sicker adults in each of these nations, especially concerning errors, communication with physicians and coordination of care. "Sicker British adults reported problems with waiting times and other non-financial barriers to care, but they were the most satisfied with their health care system." Physician shortages and long waiting times were of greatest concern to sicker adults in Australia, Canada and New Zealand. Sicker Americans were most concerned about insurance coverage, costs and financial barriers to care and, because of these concerns, were more likely to forego medical treatment, not follow up on treatment recommendations and skip medications. And all is not perfect in Germany. Rising costs, declining fertility rates and high unemployment created large budget shortfalls, recently leading to the enactment of a controversial reform by Chancellor [Angela] Merkel's coalition government that was widely resisted by unions, health insurance company employees and health care providers and came close to fracturing her coalition government.

Cost Comparisons and Health Outcomes

Certainly, efforts should be made to avoid or correct such shortcomings but, rather than comparing problems, comparing outcomes and results is more illuminating. Here, the data shows that other industrial nations spend less, cover virtually their entire populations and get better results.

Comparative data published by the Organization for Economic Co-operation and Development (OECD)—a 30-member association of industrial capitalist democracies—indicate that by nearly any measure, the United States spends far more on health care than other member nations. In 2004 the United States devoted 15.3% of GDP to health care compared to the OECD median of 8.65%—11.6% in Switzerland, 10.3% in Germany, 10.5% in France, 9.9% in Canada, 9.1% in Sweden, 8.3% in the United Kingdom, 8.0% in Australia and 8.0% in Japan. Per capita U.S. health care spending was more than twice the OECD average, $6,102 compared to $2,550. Per capita spending in Luxembourg was $5,089, in Switzerland $4,077 and in Norway $3,966. The per capita spending for each of the remaining 26 nations fell below $3,332—$3,166 in Canada, $3,005 in Germany (in 2002), $2,876 in Australia, $2,825 in Sweden, $2,249 in Japan (in 2003) and $2,546 in the United Kingdom. The United States also devotes a much larger share of its national health dollar to insurance administration expenses—7.3% in 2003 compared to 5.6% in Germany, 3.3% in the United Kingdom, 2.6% in Canada, 2.1% in Japan and 1.9% in France [according to the Commonwealth Fund].

Despite devoting a larger proportion of GDP and spending more per capita, on "key health outcome measures, U.S. performance is average or below average." In a recent study funded by the Commonwealth Fund, the United States ranked 15th out of 19 nations on a measure of "mortality from conditions that are preventable or treatable with timely, effective medical care." Forty percent of Americans compared to 9% of the British and 17% of Canadians report access problems due to the financial cost of care. Further, care is not well coordinated, in part because only "42% of Americans have been with the same physician for five years or more, compared with nearly three-fourths of patients in other countries." As is well known, similar disparities exist when the United States is compared to other nations with respect to infant mortality, with the United States ranking 23rd from the top out of 28 OECD nations reporting such data in 2003. The same is true for life expectancies at birth, with U.S. females and males both ranking 23rd out of 30 OECD nations.

Given the relatively low ranking on many health indicators, large costs and a health insurance "system" that engenders insecurity and differential access, it is not surprising that satisfaction with the U.S. health care system is declining. Although outstanding *medicine* is available for many in the United States and the United States leads the world in the development of biomedical interventions, dissatisfaction with the nation's health care *system* has doubled since 1998 [claims Ruth Helman et al. for EBRI in 2006]. Especially concerning is that the percentage of survey respondents "rating the system as poor has doubled," from 15% in 1998 to 31% in 2006. Even so, "half of Americans are *extremely* or *very* satisfied with health care quality (52%)." But "fewer than two in ten are satisfied with the cost of health insurance or with costs not covered by insurance (16% each)."

Moreover, comparisons based on two surveys of patients in Australia, Canada, Germany, New Zealand, the United Kingdom and the United States rank the United States last on four dimensions of care—patient-centeredness, efficiency, patient safety and equity; third on timeliness; and first on prevention. The research team, led by health economist Karen Davis, president and CEO of the Commonwealth Fund, concludes that "if the health care system is to perform according to patients' expectations, the U.S. will need to remove financial barriers to care and improve the delivery of care. Disparities in terms of access to services signal the need to expand insurance to cover the uninsured and to ensure that the system works well for all Americans."

The bottom line is that while the health care systems of other industrial nations have their problems, because of their smaller expenditures, they have considerably more leeway to address these problems than the U.S. system. And, most importantly, they provide access to health care to all their citizens.

Less Money, Better Outcomes

Whatever approach is taken to reforming the health care system, costs will be a major concern and potential roadblock. The bad news is that by 2016, without reform, total health care expenditures are projected to double to $4.1 trillion, and total out-of-pocket payments will go from $250 billion to $440 trillion. The hopeful news is that there are numerous documented options for slowing these increases without affecting the quality of health care. Indeed, studies have shown that spending less sometimes can improve the quality of health care outcomes.

The potential for savings is huge. The Commonwealth Fund states that

> the effect of achieving a one-time reduction in the level of health care spending by 5% in 2007 would achieve cumulative savings over the eight year period from 2007 to 2015 of $1.31 trillion. Just lowering the rate of health care increases by one percent a year would save $1.39 trillion over the same time period.

Roadblocks to achieving such savings include the powerful interests that profit from the current system, in addition to Americans' strong belief that you get what you pay for, the tendency to measure the quality of health care in terms of inputs (new technology, new drugs) rather than outcomes (the results of interactions with the health care system) and a lack of understanding how health care dollars are spent.

Our purpose here is not to present a comprehensive review of the options for containing health care costs and expenditures, but to provide some examples of how health care spending can be reduced without affecting quality care and in some cases improving health care outcomes. First, it will be important to clarify the goals of cost containment. We suggest that proposed reform measures be evaluated in part by how well they advance the following goals:

- Bring the rate of increases in total health care expenditures more in line with rate of inflation.
- Ensure affordable health care coverage for all, including slowing the rates at which health insurance premiums have been increasing.
- Improve the nation's quality of care.

Outcomes research, a relatively new area of study in medicine, has identified widespread inefficient or ineffective uses of care and practices that reduce costs and improve quality. For example, the *Dartmouth Atlas of Health Care* documents the wide range of per capita Medicare health care spending in different parts of the country with no impact on longevity or the quality of care delivered. The range of spending per beneficiary stretched from $4,503 in Hawaii to $8,080 in New Jersey. Wider use of best practices would reduce the amount spent on unwarranted variations in the delivery of care.

A project that is testing paying hospitals for performance (outcomes) rather than for inputs (treatments) found that the incentive had resulted in improved quality and reduced costs.

A change in the administration of antibiotics to surgical patients "significantly reduced post-operative deep wound infections, thus saving money and improving quality" [writes Caryl E. Carpenter et al. in a 1996 issue of *Quality in Health Care*].

A study of the records of 4.7 million Medicare beneficiaries, who died between 2000 and 2003 and had a chronic illness, found that almost one-third of the $120 billion spent on the patients over the four years was unnecessary and did not improve quality of care [a 2006 Dartmouth Medical Project paper reported].

In the words of Donald M. Berwick, M.D., a leading national authority on health care quality and improvement issues, "The nation can do a lot to improve the quality and lower the cost of health care once providers, policy makers, payers and the public share an understanding that 'more care' is not by any means always 'better care' and that new technologies and hospital stays can sometimes harm more than help."

Reducing Overhead Spending

And then there are the administrative overhead charges paid to private insurance companies out of health care insurance premiums. A recently released study estimates that when compared to administrative costs paid by residents of France, Finland and

More Care at Half the Cost

Universal health care is in place throughout the industrialized world. In most cases, doctors and hospitals operate as private businesses. But government pays the bills, which reduces paperwork costs to a fraction of the American level. It also cuts out expensive insurance corporations and HMOs, with their multimillion-dollar CEO compensation packages, and billions in profit. Small wonder "single payer" systems can cover their entire populations at half the per capita cost.

Doug Pibel and Sarah van Gelder, "Health Care: It's What Ails Us," Yes! Magazine, *July 19, 2006. www.yesmagazine.org.*

Japan, U.S. residents spend $97 billion a year in excessive administrative charges to insurance companies. The study did not estimate the administrative costs incurred by practitioners forced to deal with multiple insurance carriers. Much of the $97 billion goes for marketing and underwriting, expenses that would not be incurred under a single-payer system. Savings from reduced overhead spending would offset the cost of providing full health care coverage to the uninsured, estimated to cost $77 billion a year. Moreover, as the *New York Times* editorialized, "eliminating the large overpayments granted to private health plans that participate in Medicare would save $65 billion over five years."

And finally there is the issue of the increasing price of drugs. For the last decade, the drug industry, by its own figures, has spent about 2.5 times more money on marketing and administration than on research. Further, [as Marcia Angell stated in a 2004 issue of the *New York Review of Books*] in 2002 "the combined profits for ten drug companies in the Fortune 500 ($35.9 billion) were more than the profits for all the other 490 businesses ($33.7 billion)." There seems to be ample room for reducing the prices on drugs without reducing investments in research.

In short, the data prove that there are ample opportunities to contain health care expenditures and the costs of health care insurance while, in many cases, improving the quality of care. There are enough potential savings to more than finance a national health insurance program covering everyone.

Universal Coverage Is a Moral Imperative

Universal access to health care is the practical road to health care reform in terms of improved quality and cost containment, but more importantly it is the right thing to do. At the most fundamental level, universal access should be a moral imperative, a right of citizenship in any country that can afford it, no different from public safety protections and access to primary and secondary education and libraries. It is a basic human right, not a commodity to be bartered in the marketplace, to be made available based on class, race and social position. Its "commoditization" diminishes patients, health care providers and the community.

No doubt, even in a wealthy nation, favorable health outcomes reflect relative privilege, but not to the extent that it does in the United States. It is not defensible for this nation to allow widely inequitable health care access and services to its population. It is not acceptable that health care outcomes are skewed by education, class, race and ethnicity—with the U.S. Agency for Healthcare Research and Quality reporting in its 2006 *National Healthcare Disparities Report* that the poor and racial and ethnic minorities generally have less access to care and receive a lower quality of care. Also unacceptable is that, when compared to white Americans, African Americans experience age-adjusted death rates from cancer that are 25%

greater, age-adjusted death rates from diabetes that are more than 100% greater and infant mortality rates that are 130% greater.

No doubt incentives have an important role to play in restructuring the American health care system, for example, incentives to encourage healthier lifestyles. But, the health care market is fundamentally different from consumer markets for such items as clothing, automobiles and housing.

Persons needing health care are not well positioned to "haggle" over prices, judge quality or make decisions about how to compare prices and assess the quality of lower priced care (especially when "gowned" in a treatment room!). Faced with serious health problems, demand is inelastic and patients look to expert opinions regarding treatments, referrals, pharmaceuticals and care settings, often regardless of costs. Third-party payments further the need for government to provide countervailing pressure on costs. And counterintuitive to market logic, there is evidence that, within a geographic location, use of medical care often expands to meet the supply of medical care available, with little or no reductions in costs or improvements in quality. Most important, markets do not distribute access to health care in an equitable manner, leaving many without insurance coverage and leading to unacceptable health outcomes and disparities across "have" and "have not" populations.

The argument for universal access to quality health care goes well beyond the successful experiences of other nations— showing it can be done at costs well below ours. It is good that they succeed where we do not. It is good, too, that potential efficiencies and expenditure savings can be made in our health care system by reducing paperwork, by application of health information technology, by wellness approaches and by making consumers more aware of the cost of care and benefits of generics. And it is good that an expanded role for government in the nation's health care system holds the promise of greater efficiency and cost control.

But, at the core, a society such as ours—that aspires to treat each life with dignity [and] is based on democratic principles that give expression to widely held religious values such as caring for our parents, our neighbors and community—can accept no less than a decent standard of care for all its members. And universal access to health care is fundamentally in partnership with a just, competitive economy. As change engenders greater likelihood of job shifts over the course of workers' lives; as the nation's occupationally based health and employer pension systems become less certain and private retiree health benefits diminish; as the rising cost of health care premiums becomes more burdensome to families and undermines the international competitiveness of employers, it is increasingly important that citizens be assured through democratic institutions that their own and their family's health care is not subject to the vagaries of employment or income position.

A Society Based on Social Responsibility

Princeton economist and Provost J. Douglas Brown (1898–1986), an architect of the Social Security Act of 1935, spoke eloquently of an implied covenant in social insurance programs such as Social Security, Medicare and national health insurance, arising from a deeply embedded sense of mutual responsibility in civilization. This covenant, he wrote, underlies the fundamental obligation of the government and citizens of one time and the government and citizens of another time to maintain a contributory social insurance system.

Ultimately, universal access to health care is grounded in values of concern for all members of society and in shared responsibility. It reflects an understanding of the social compact that, as citizens and human beings, we are "all in it together"; we all share certain risks and certain vulnerabilities; and we all have a stake in advancing practical mechanisms of self- and mutual support. It reflects a positive vision that government—

working in partnership with the private sector and citizens—can and should uphold these values by providing practical, dignified, secure and efficient means for Americans to protect their children, families and themselves against health risks to which all are subject.

> "[The US health care system] is not
> inferior to other developed countries'
> systems—and we should therefore
> not be looking to these systems,
> most of which are characterized by
> heavy government intervention, for
> inspiration."

America Does Not Need Universal Health Care

John C. Goodman

In the viewpoint that follows, John C. Goodman claims that arguments for universal health care in the United States are based on faulty assumptions. Goodman asserts that American health care is equal to or better than its counterparts in other developed nations with universal care. He maintains that, in America, waiting times for services are typically shorter and survival rates for common diseases such as cancer and diabetes are higher. He also insists Americans have easy access to health care (even government-assisted health care) and that a significant portion of the uninsured go without coverage by choice, not circumstance. For these reasons, he sees no advantage in adopting nationalized health care. John C. Goodman is the CEO of the National Center for Policy Analysis, a nonprofit conservative think tank.

John C. Goodman, "Socialized Failure," *National Review*, vol. 61, no. 9, May 25, 2009. Used by permission.

As you read, consider the following questions:

1. Why does Goodman believe it is unfair to utilize life expectancy and infant mortality rates as a standard of comparison between the health care systems in the United States and Europe?

2. According to the author, how many Britons are waiting for hospital or outpatient treatment at any given time?

3. What percent of uninsured "spells" for Americans last fewer than two years, as Goodman claims?

The health-care systems of all developed countries face three unrelenting problems: rising costs, inadequate quality, and incomplete access to care. A slew of recent articles, published mainly in medical journals, suggest that the health-care systems of other countries are superior to ours on all these fronts. Yet the articles are at odds with a substantial economic literature.

What follows is a brief review of the evidence. As other writers demonstrate elsewhere in this issue, the American health-care system has plenty of problems. But it is not inferior to other developed countries' systems—and we should therefore not be looking to these systems, most of which are characterized by heavy government intervention, for inspiration.

Does the United States Spend More on Health Care?

Taken at face value, international statistics show that the United States spends more than twice as much per person on health care as the average developed country. But these statistics are misleading. Other countries are far more aggressive than we are at disguising and shifting costs—for example, by using the power of government purchase to artificially suppress the incomes of doctors, nurses, and hospital personnel. This makes their aggregate outlays look smaller when all that has really happened is that part of the cost has been shifted from one group (patients and

Another Example of Misplaced Faith in a Benevolent Government

Many Utopian dreamers are motivated by the best of intentions and envision that the best way to achieve high quality health care is to create a system by which the government will control all health care spending and ensure that it is equitable, efficient and proper. They are basing their approach on an economic philosophy that has failed many times in history—one of collectivism and central economic planning. Many of those advocating such a system believe that if an elite group of all knowing and benevolent planners control spending, that nothing but good will result. Unfortunately this had never been the case as evidenced by the fall of the Berlin Wall, the lack of property and individual rights in societies under dictators, and recent examples of failing government-run school systems in America with a never-ending supply of money.

David McKalip, "The Trouble with 'Single-Payer Healthcare,'" Campaign for Liberty, May 12, 2009. www.campaignforliberty.com.

taxpayers) to another (health-care providers). This is equivalent to taxing doctors, nurses, or some other group so that others may pay less for their care.

Normal market forces have been so suppressed throughout the developed world that the prices paid for medical services rarely reflect the services' actual cost. As a result, adding all these prices together produces aggregate numbers in which one can have little confidence. One gets a better measure of how much countries spend by looking at the real resources used; and by that measure, the U.S. system is pretty good. For example, we use fewer doctors than the average developed country to produce the same or better outcomes. We also use fewer nurses and fewer hospital beds, make fewer physician visits, and spend fewer days in the hospital. About the only thing we use more of is technology.

Spending *totals* aside, the U.S. has been neither worse nor better than the rest of the developed world at controlling spending *growth*. The average annual rate of growth of real per capita U.S. health-care spending is slightly below the OECD [Organization for Economic Co-operation and Development] average over the past four decades (4.4 percent versus 4.5 percent). It appears that other developed countries are traveling down the same spending path we are.

Are U.S. Health Outcomes Worse?

Critics point to the fact that U.S. life expectancy is in the middle of the pack among developed countries, and that our infant-mortality rate is among the highest. But are these the right measures? Within the U.S., life expectancy at birth varies greatly between racial and ethnic groups, from state to state, and across counties. These differences are thought to reflect such lifestyle choices as diet, exercise, and smoking. Infant mortality varies by a factor of two or three across racial and ethnic lines, and from city to city and state to state, for reasons apparently having little to do with health care.

All too often, the heterogeneous population of the United States is compared with the homogeneous populations of European countries. A state such as Utah compares favorably with almost any developed country. Texas, with its high minority population, tends to compare unfavorably. But these outcomes have almost nothing to do with the doctors and hospitals in the two states.

It makes far more sense to look at the diseases and conditions to which we know medical science can make a real difference—cancer, diabetes, and hypertension, for example. The largest international study to date found that the five-year survival rate for all types of cancer among both men and women was higher in the U.S. than in Europe. There is a steeper increase in blood pressure with advancing age in Europe, and a 60 percent higher prevalence of hypertension. The aggressive treatment offered to U.S. cardiac patients apparently improves survival and functioning relative to that of Canadian patients. Fewer health- and disability-related problems occur among U.S. spinal-cord-injury patients than among Canadian and British patients.

Do Patients in Other Countries Have Better Access to Care?

Britain has only one-fourth as many CT scanners per capita as the U.S. and one-third as many MRI scanners. The rate at which the British provide coronary-bypass surgery or angioplasty to heart patients is only one-fourth the U.S. rate, and hip replacements are only two-thirds the U.S. rate. The rate for treating kidney failure (dialysis or transplant) is five times higher in the U.S. for patients between the ages of 45 and 84, and nine times higher for patients 85 years or older.

Overall, nearly 1.8 million Britons are waiting for hospital or outpatient treatments at any given time. In 2002–2004, dialysis patients waited an average of 16 days for permanent blood-vessel access in the U.S., 20 days in Europe, and 62 days in Canada. In 2000, Norwegian patients waited an average of 133 days for hip replacement, 63 days for cataract surgery, 160 days for a knee replacement, and 46 days for bypass surgery after being approved for treatment. Short waits for cataract surgery produce better outcomes, prompt coronary-artery bypass reduces mortality, and rapid hip replacement reduces disability and death. Studies show that only 5 percent of Americans wait more than four months for surgery, compared with 23 percent of Australians, 26 percent of New Zealanders, 27 percent of Canadians, and 36 percent of Britons.

Do Other Countries Do a Better Job of Delivering Preventive Care?

If people have to pay for care directly, it is often claimed, they will be inclined to skimp on preventive care—care that can catch

diseases in their early stages, saving lives and money. Yet the proportion of middle-aged Canadian women who have never had a
mammogram is twice that of the U.S., and three times as many
Canadian women have never had a Pap smear. Fewer than a fifth
of Canadian men have ever been tested for prostate-specific antigen, compared with about half of American men. Only one in ten
adult Canadians has had a colonoscopy, compared with about a
third of adult Americans.

These differences in screening may partly explain why the
mortality rate in Canada is 25 percent higher for breast cancer,
18 percent higher for prostate cancer, and 13 percent higher for
colorectal cancer. In addition, while half of all diabetics have
high blood pressure, it is controlled in 36 percent of U.S. cases,
compared with only 9 percent of cases in Canada.

Do the Uninsured in the United States
Lack Access to Health Care?

Of the 46 million nominally uninsured, about 12 million are
eligible for such public programs as Medicaid and the State
Children's Health Insurance Program (S-CHIP). They can usually enroll even at the time of treatment, arguably making them
de facto insured. About 17 million of the uninsured are living in
households with annual incomes of at least $50,000. More than
half of those earn more than $75,000, suggesting that they are
uninsured by choice.

Like unemployment, uninsurance is usually transitory:
75 percent of uninsured spells last one year or less, and 91 percent last two years or less. Although the fraction of the population with health insurance rises and falls with the business
cycle, it has been fairly constant for the past two decades,
despite an unprecedented influx of immigrants with an uninsurance rate 2.5 times that of the native-born population.
Guaranteed-issue laws, state high-risk pools, and retroactive
Medicaid eligibility make it increasingly easy to obtain insurance after becoming ill.

Are Low-Income Families More Disadvantaged in the U.S. System?

Aneurin Bevan, father of the British National Health Service (NHS), declared, "The essence of a satisfactory health service is that rich and poor are treated alike, that poverty is not a disability and wealth is not advantaged." More than 30 years after the NHS's founding, an official task force found little evidence that it had equalized health-care access. Another study, 20 years later, concluded that access had become more unequal in the years between the two studies.

In Canada, the wealthy and powerful have significantly greater access to medical specialists than do the less well-connected poor. High-profile patients enjoy more frequent services, shorter waiting times, and greater choice of specialists. Moreover, non-elderly, white, low-income Canadians are 22 percent more likely to be in poor health than their U.S. counterparts.

In developed countries generally, among people with similar health conditions, high earners use the system more intensely, and use costlier services, than do low earners. It seems likely that the personal characteristics that ensure success in a market economy also enhance success in bureaucratic systems.

| "Letting Americans control their health care dollars and breaking up the states' monopolies on insurance and clinician licensing . . . would put access to health care within reach of millions of Americans."

Free-Market Competition Can Fix Rising Health Care Costs

Michael F. Cannon

Michael F. Cannon is the director of health care policy studies at the Cato Institute, a libertarian public policy research organization. In the following viewpoint, Cannon argues against more government-run health care and instead advocates the establishment of free-market principles within the system. Cannon believes that a market-driven approach will encourage competition, which will, in turn, drive down prices while giving consumers more choice in how to provide for their own health care. He asserts that health care should be portable across state borders, thus eliminating insurance and clinician licensing monopolies and forcing states to improve their consumer protections to match competition from providers in other states. Cannon further argues that the resulting lower health care costs would mean that states and the federal

Michael F. Cannon, "Yes, Mr. President: A Free Market Can Fix Health Care," *Cato Policy Analysis*, no. 650, October 21, 2009. Used by permission.

government would have more money to address the health needs of
those who cannot afford health care of any type.

As you read, consider the following questions:

1. Why is the federal tax code unfair to Americans who want
   to purchase their own health insurance directly from providers, according to Cannon?
2. In Cannon's opinion, why would giving consumers control over their health care spending not likely lead individuals to skimp on care?
3. According to the Congressional Budget Office, as cited by
   the author, how much do state insurance regulations raise
   the price of premiums on average?

At present, America's health care sector is far from a free
market. Government directly controls nearly half of all
health care spending, and indirectly controls most of the remainder. Government controls more than half of the nation's
health *insurance* dollars (through Medicare, Medicaid, and
other public programs), and delegates control over another third
to employers through the preferential tax treatment granted to
employer-sponsored health insurance. The federal government
imposes an average tax penalty of more than 40 percent on the
one market that offers a wide range of health plans and seamless coverage between jobs: the "individual" market, where consumers purchase coverage directly from insurers. (Indeed, that
tax penalty may explain much public dissatisfaction with the
individual market.) More than half of U.S. health care spending takes place under government price and exchange controls. As President [Barack] Obama's economic adviser Larry
Summers reminds us, "Price and exchange controls inevitably
create harmful economic distortions. Both the distortions and
the economic damage get worse with time." That is to say nothing of the countless counterproductive regulations that govern-

ment imposes on clinicians, insurance, medical products, and health care facilities.

As health economist Victor Fuchs explains, most leading health care reforms "aim at cost shifting rather than cost reduction." Whereas the legislation that President Obama is shepherding through Congress [i.e., the Patient Protection and Affordable Care Act] attempts to cover the uninsured by pouring more resources into health care, a free market would get more out of America's health care sector. Letting Americans control their health care dollars and breaking up the states' monopolies on insurance and clinician licensing (with "regulatory federalism") would put access to health care within reach of millions of Americans by putting downward pressure on health care prices and health insurance premiums. Those reforms would also dramatically improve quality by allowing various health plans, with various payment systems and delivery systems, to compete on a level playing field.

Wasting Health Care Dollars

Health care spending is growing unsustainably. Over the past 30 years, health care spending has grown more than 2 percentage points faster than the economy overall, and now stands at 18 percent of GDP [gross domestic product].

That would not be a problem if we were getting our money's worth. The most credible estimates, however, suggest an alarming one-third of health care spending does nothing to make patients healthier or happier. In 2009, Americans will waste more than $800 billion—about 6 percent of U.S. GDP—on medical care that provides zero benefit to patients. Americans will waste additional billions on services whose benefits are not worth the cost. That wasteful spending results in higher taxes, higher health insurance premiums, and more uninsured Americans.

Government is largely incapable of eliminating wasteful health care spending, because nobody spends other people's money as carefully as they spend their own. Government tax and entitlement policy denies patients ownership of their health care dollars, and thereby strips [government] of any incentive to control costs. Due to federal tax policy, for example, Stanford University health economist Alain Enthoven estimates that "less than 5 percent of the insured workforce can both choose a health plan and reap the full savings from choosing economically." Indeed, consumers resist efforts to eliminate wasteful spending, and with good reason. Since they are enjoying health insurance that is effectively purchased with other people's money, consumers receive no direct financial benefit from eliminating wasteful spending, whether through cost-sharing or care management. When Medicare tries to eliminate coverage of low-value services or to reduce excessive provider payments, seniors experience nothing but pain. Workers perceive increased cost-sharing or managed-care controls as cuts in their compensation. Even though these steps should ultimately lead to higher wages and lower taxes, those benefits are not salient to seniors and workers.

That lack of cost-consciousness creates what author David Goldhill describes as "an accidental collusion between providers benefiting from higher costs and patients who don't fully bear them." Former Senate Majority Leader Tom Daschle writes that this results in a politically powerful "patient-provider pincer movement" that blocks efforts to reduce wasteful spending. The patient-provider pincer movement prevents Medicare from considering cost-effectiveness when deciding whether to cover particular services; repeatedly eliminates funding for federal agencies that conduct comparative-effectiveness research; preserves excessive Medicare payments for specialists, insurers, and procedures; blocks competitive bidding for durable medical equipment in Medicare; has made a joke out of the scheduled "sustainable-growth-rate" cuts to Medicare physician payments; and even curtails private-sector efforts to eliminate wasteful spending with managed-care controls.

The end result is that both government- and employer-sponsored insurance waste money in ways that consumers spending their own money never would. If the health reform legislation currently before Congress becomes law, politicians and employers will continue to control Americans' health care dollars, and this government failure will persist.

The Free-Market Alternative

A free market, in contrast, would eliminate wasteful health care spending. Individuals would control their own health care dollars and would therefore benefit directly from reducing waste. A less-regulated market would also free Americans to choose from a wide variety of health plans and providers.

When consumers own and control their health care dollars—in particular, the money that purchases their health insurance—the self-interest of hundreds of millions of Americans will lead them to choose health plans that eliminate wasteful spending, whether through cost-sharing or care management, in exchange for lower premiums. Peter Orszag, President Obama's director of the Office of Management and Budget, testified before Congress on the promise of individual ownership:

> Workers may demand less efficiency from the health system than they would if they knew the full cost that they pay via forgone wages for coverage or if they knew the actual cost of the services being provided.
>
> [I]magine what the world would be like if workers [understood] that today it was costing them $10,000 a year in take-home pay for their employer-sponsored insurance, and that could be $7,000 and they could have $3,000 more in their pockets today if we could relieve these inefficiencies out of the health system. Making those costs more transparent may generate demand for efficiency.

Consumers who *own* the money they are spending are a cornerstone of free and functional markets. A free market would reduce wasteful spending with minimal harm because, unlike price controls and other tools of government rationing, markets allocate resources according to consumer preferences, rather than the preferences of politicians, government bureaucrats, or special-interest lobbyists.

Restoring individual ownership to health care will require a two-pronged strategy.

Medicare Vouchers

For Americans covered by Medicare, Congress should give enrollees a voucher and let them choose any health plan available on the market. To ensure that all beneficiaries can afford a basic health plan, Medicare should give larger vouchers to poorer and sicker seniors and smaller vouchers to healthy and wealthy seniors, using current health-risk-adjustment mechanisms and Social Security data on lifetime earnings.

The amount of each individual's voucher must be fixed, so that enrollees who want to purchase comprehensive coverage would have to pay more for it. Likewise, if a Medicare enrollee chooses an economical policy, she could save the balance of her voucher in an account dedicated to out-of-pocket medical expenses. When enrollees bear the added cost of comprehensive coverage, and reap the savings from more economical coverage, their self-interest will lead them to select health plans that curb wasteful spending. Letting seniors make their own rationing decisions is the only way to protect seniors from government rationing.

Reforming Tax Breaks

In the film *Sicko*, director Michael Moore took five Ground Zero rescue workers to Cuba, where they received "free" treatment for the ailments they contracted during the 9/11 rescue effort. All five had employer-sponsored insurance on September 11, 2001, but lost their coverage when they subsequently lost those jobs. Had they been free to purchase coverage directly from an insurance company without penalty, Moore would have had more difficulty finding sick, uninsured Americans.

To give people under age 65 the freedom to control their health care dollars without penalty, Congress must reform the tax code. Employer-provided health insurance currently receives favorable tax treatment compared to health insurance that consumers purchase directly. That tax preference reduces the after-tax price of employer-sponsored insurance by 30 percent on average, which is the equivalent of imposing a 42-percent tax penalty on coverage purchased directly from an insurance company. As a result, some 163 million non-elderly Americans obtain coverage through an employer, while only 18 million purchase coverage directly from an insurance company. The "tax exclusion" for employer-sponsored insurance encourages wasteful health spending by also distorting the after-tax price of medical services relative to other uses of income.

This supposed tax "break" for employer-sponsored health insurance actually operates more like a tax hike, because it denies workers control over a large portion of their earnings as well as their health care decisions. To obtain this tax break in 2009, workers with self-only coverage sacrificed control over more than $4,000 of their earnings to their employers, while those with family coverage sacrificed control of nearly $10,000, on average. Analysts typically call those amounts the "employer contribution" to the cost of health benefits, yet economists agree that employers fund those contributions by reducing workers' wages. In other words, that money is part of each worker's earnings, but the worker does not and cannot control it. This tax break also largely confines workers' coverage choices to the few (if any) options their employer offers. In 2008, 80 percent of covered workers had at most two health insurance options; 47 percent had only one option.

The tax preference for employer-sponsored insurance therefore creates a health insurance "market" that largely resembles a government program. Much like a tax, it denies workers control over their earnings. Much like a government program, it empowers agents—that is, employers—to determine whether consumers will have a choice of health plans, and what those choices will be. As with government programs, federal nondiscrimination rules effectively impose price controls that prohibit insurance premiums from varying according to risk.

Let Consumers Take Advantage of an Equitable Tax Code

Returning those earnings to the workers requires reforming the tax code so that all health insurance—whether purchased through an employer or directly from an insurer—receives the same tax treatment. For example, replacing the current tax exclusion with either health-insurance tax credits, a standard deduction for health insurance, or large health savings accounts [HSAs] would level the playing field between employment-based coverage and other sources of health insurance. Absent any tax preference for employer-sponsored coverage, workers could demand that employers give them their $4,000 or $10,000 as cash, and could use those funds to purchase coverage from any source. A competitive labor market would force employers to comply.

All of which means that eliminating the tax preference for job-based insurance would be an enormous tax *cut*. First and most obvious, the above-mentioned tax reforms would provide tax breaks to all individuals, regardless of where they purchase health insurance. Those reforms would therefore deliver tax relief to individuals who purchase insurance outside an employment setting, and who currently receive no tax break.

Second, and less obvious, eliminating the tax preference for employer-sponsored insurance would result in a massive tax cut for workers with employer-sponsored insurance, because each insured worker would gain control over $4,000 or $10,000 of her earnings that she currently does not control. In 2007, employers contributed more than $532 billion to employee health benefits. In the prior 10 years, aggregate employer contributions grew at an average rate of 8 percent. Assuming that they continue to grow at that rate through 2019, employer contributions to employee health benefits will total $9.7 trillion over the next 10 years.

Eliminating the tax preference for employer-sponsored insurance would therefore shift control over more than $532 billion each year, and $9.7 trillion over the next 10 years, from employers to workers. That effective $9.7 trillion tax cut would not increase the federal budget deficit, and it would more than swamp any small, explicit tax increases that altering the existing tax treatment of employer-sponsored insurance would impose on some insured workers. Unlike other tax reforms, large HSAs would deliver that tax cut immediately and with greater transparency. . . .

Allaying Common Fears

Few dispute that letting consumers control their health care dollars would reduce wasteful health care spending. The most common criticism of individual ownership is that consumers would restrain spending too much; that many consumers would skimp on care, leading to higher costs down the road. Research suggests that is not the case. The RAND Health Insurance Experiment showed that either cost-sharing or care management can reduce wasteful health care spending without harming overall health. Individual ownership and greater competition could even improve health by expanding access to health plans that emphasize preventive care, coordinated care, information technologies (including electronic medical records), medical-error reduction, and comparative-effectiveness research.

Critics also fear that, in the transition from the current tax preference for employer-sponsored insurance to a level playing field, some workers with high-cost illnesses would be unable to obtain coverage. If enough workers leave an employer's health plan for the individual market, the employer may have to drop its health benefits. The sickest people in those pools would then have difficulty purchasing coverage on their own.

For several reasons, this serious concern should not be an obstacle to letting workers control their own money. First, thousands of workers are already losing their employer-sponsored insurance with every passing day, because employers are either dropping coverage or eliminating jobs. Many have expensive illnesses and are subsequently unable to purchase coverage. They generally receive no tax breaks to help them purchase private health insurance. Tax reform would assist those workers by reducing the after-tax cost of coverage for everyone who purchases insurance on the individual market.

Second, the freedom to purchase health insurance directly from an insurance company—coverage that stays with consumers between jobs—will guarantee that fewer Americans would find themselves in such dire straits. . . .

Third, the individual market does a better job of providing health insurance to the sick than conventional wisdom suggests. [Economist Mark] Pauly, Susan Marquis of the RAND Corporation, and their respective colleagues find that there is significant subsidization of the sick by the healthy in the individual market, and that such pooling increases over time. Contrary to the conventional wisdom, Marquis and colleagues find that in California's individual market, "a large number of people with health problems do obtain coverage."

Fourth, the above-mentioned tax reforms would put relatively more money in the hands of workers with higher medical costs. Economists consistently find that cash wages adjust downward to account for the higher costs that older, obese, and female employees impose on an employer's health plan. Put differently, workers with costly medical conditions accept lower wages than they could otherwise command, in order to obtain health benefits.

Those workers would therefore receive the biggest tax cuts after eliminating the tax preference for employer-sponsored insurance. The fact that those workers currently accept lower wages than they could otherwise command means that they would generally receive more than the average $4,000 or $10,000 annual cash-out. . . .

Breaking up Monopolies to Make Coverage Affordable

Making health insurance more affordable requires more than giving consumers control over their health care dollars. Government regulations drive health care costs higher by blocking competition from more-efficient providers, insurance plans, delivery systems—and even more-efficient regulators. Reforming insurance and clinician regulation with "regulatory federalism" would make health insurance more affordable, as well as expand the freedom to choose one's own doctor and health plan.

Monopolistic Insurance Licensing

State health-insurance licensing is a prime example of costly regulation. Each state requires insurers to obtain a license from that state's government in order to sell insurance within that state's borders. Those laws effectively give each state a monopoly over providing consumer protections to insurance purchasers because they prevent employers and individuals from purchasing health insurance licensed and regulated by other states.

Some form of regulation is necessary to ensure that health insurers keep their commitments to their enrollees. Yet monopolistic insurance-licensing laws may be more harmful than helpful. Those laws give government the power to dictate the terms of every health insurance policy sold in the state—a power that is inevitably captured by the health care industry.

As a result, state insurance-licensing laws require consumers to purchase coverage for an average of 42 specific types of health services—whether the consumer wants that coverage or not. Some states also use insurance-licensing laws to enact price controls that tax healthy consumers to subsidize the sick. Those price-control laws typically do little to increase risk pooling, but they do create perverse incentives for insurers to avoid the sick and can cause insurance markets to unravel. Physicians have used insurance-licensing laws to protect their incomes from market forces that would otherwise make health care more affordable. The

Congressional Budget Office estimates that state health insurance regulations increase health insurance premiums by 15 percent on average. Eliminating just half of that burden could save families $1,000 or more on their premiums.

Monopolistic Clinician Licensing

Regulation increases health care costs by blocking competition between clinicians as well. As with insurance, each state requires clinicians to obtain a license from that state's government in order to practice within its borders. Those clinician-licensing laws define a "scope of practice" for each type of mid-level clinician, such as nurse practitioners and physician assistants. Those laws give government the power to decide what tasks each type of clinician may perform. Again, that power is inevitably captured by the health care industry—in this case, by competing clinicians, especially physicians.

Clinicians' scopes of practice are a perennial battleground for clinician groups who try to block competition for their members by narrowing the range of services that competing clinicians perform, or the settings in which they practice. Ophthalmologists use licensing laws to prevent optometrists from performing surgical procedures. Anesthesiologists use licensing laws to block competition from nurse anesthetists. Physicians use licensing laws to prevent podiatrists from treating the ankle, as well as to restrict nurse practitioners' ability to prescribe drugs and operate retail clinics. Physicians have even used clinician-licensing laws to block competition from health insurers that contain costs by making more extensive use of mid-level clinicians (e.g., physician assistants, nurse practitioners). There is ample evidence that clinician-licensing laws have increased costs by blocking competition, yet there is little or no evidence that such laws have made patients any healthier. . . .

Break up Regulatory Monopolies

Consumer protections are ultimately a product. Like all monopolies, the monopolies that state governments hold over licensing clinicians and insurers produce high-cost, low-quality consumer protections. The most promising way to spur cost-saving competition between clinicians and insurers is to break up those monopolies and force regulators to compete to provide the best set of consumer protections.

With regard to insurance, that means preventing states from using their insurance-licensing laws as a barrier to entry for insurance products licensed by other states. An employer or consumer in Michigan, for example, should be allowed to purchase an insurance policy licensed in Connecticut or any other state, so that the only insurance regulations that would govern that relationship would be Connecticut's. Those regulations could be incorporated into the insurance contract, so that the purchaser could enforce Connecticut's consumer protections in Michigan courts, even with the help of Michigan's insurance commissioner. (State courts frequently enforce other states' laws already.)

Allowing state-issued insurance licenses to cross state lines would make insurance more affordable. It would give employers and individual purchasers the freedom to choose only the coverage and regulatory protections they want, and to avoid unwanted regulatory costs. A study by Stephen Parente and colleagues at the University of Minnesota estimated that ending those regulatory monopolies could cover an additional 17 million Americans, or one-third of the most commonly cited estimate of the uninsured. Moreover, it would do so without creating any new taxes or new government subsidies, and would likely reduce the federal deficit.

With regard to clinicians, breaking up regulatory monopolies means preventing state governments from barring entry to clinicians licensed by other states. Physicians and other clinicians licensed by Virginia should be able to practice in Maryland or Maine or Montana under the terms of their Virginia license, while still subject to local malpractice rules. That change would give physicians and mid-level clinicians more freedom to live and practice where they wish.

The primary benefit of ending this regulatory monopoly, however, would likely come from encouraging competition by corporate providers of care, such as retail clinics and health plans like Kaiser Permanente and Group Health Cooperative. Such providers operate their own facilities and employ their own staff of clinicians. Health plans like Kaiser and Group Health strive to make medical care more affordable, in part by using mid-level clinicians to their full competence. Making state-issued clinician licenses portable would enable such organizations to compete nationwide without facing different regulatory obstacles in each state.

Eliminating both types of regulatory monopoly would force states to compete to provide the protections that consumers demand, while avoiding unwanted regulatory costs. . . .

Market Mechanisms Would Ensure Consumer Protection

Critics fear that breaking up states' regulatory monopolies would spur states to gut essential consumer protections in an effort to capture health insurance premium taxes and clinician licensing fees. The result would be a "race to the bottom" where fly-by-night insurance companies and incompetent clinicians do harm to patients.

Yet political factors and competitive market forces would prevent a race to the bottom by restoring vital consumer protections. Suppose that Delaware gutted its consumer protections and began issuing licenses to sketchy insurers and clinicians, in the hope of collecting lots of premium taxes and licensing fees. Could Delaware get away with it? Not likely. First, some of those insurers and clinicians would inevitably harm Delaware residents, who would demand that their politicians restore those essential consumer protections. Second, competitors would discipline the low-quality clinicians and health plans licensed by Delaware. Higher-quality insurers and clinicians would advertise their credentials, including the fact that they comply with the stronger consumer protections demanded by other states. Third, courts in other states would deter Delaware-licensed insurers and clinicians from bad behavior by enforcing contracts and punishing medical negligence. Regulatory federalism would still allow each state to set its own medical malpractice rules, which provide additional (and perhaps superior) protections against incompetent clinicians. Finally, consumers themselves would discipline low-quality insurers and clinicians after learning of Delaware's reputation through the news, *Consumer Reports*, and other media. Whether Delaware eliminated vital consumer protections deliberately or inadvertently, these self-correcting mechanisms would restore those essential consumer protections. . . .

Free Market Would Create More Resources for Needy and Uninsured

A free market would provide better and more affordable health insurance to more Americans, but it would not provide health insurance to every last person. Many would require subsidized health care, either because they did not purchase health insurance when they could have, or because health insurance was never within their grasp.

The first contribution that a free market would make to alleviate the suffering of the needy would be to reduce the number of Americans who find themselves unable to afford medical care. Through greater price competition and innovation, a free market would put health insurance and medical care within the reach for more low- and middle-income Americans. It would also provide more seamless and secure health insurance coverage, so that fewer Americans would find themselves sick and uninsured.

Congress should build on the success of welfare reform by reforming those programs the same way it reformed the Aid to Families with Dependent Children program in 1996: with block grants that give states the ability and the incentive to target those resources to the truly needy. As markets make health insurance more secure and medical care more affordable, fewer people will fall into this vulnerable situation, and it will be easier to care for those who do.

| "The problems of the [health care] sector as a whole will not yield to 'free market' ideas—never will, never can."

Free-Market Competition Will Not Fix Rising Health Care Costs

Joe Flower

In the viewpoint that follows, Joe Flower, a health care speaker, writer, and consultant, argues that the US health care system cannot adopt free-market, supply-and-demand principles. As Flower claims, demand in health care is variable because not everyone suffers from the same illnesses or uses services in the same way. Therefore Flower asserts that the costs of health care must be spread around the population or they will severely impact the sickest part of society. Flower also insists that free-market values cannot work because the providers (doctors and hospitals) are both the suppliers and consultants in the market equation. That is, according to the author, doctors will have no incentive to provide fewer services (even though many will be unnecessary) and discourage patients (who seek doctors' advice) from purchasing them. Because consumers must trust in the advice of their doctors, the advantages of the market system accrue chiefly to the health care providers, Flower maintains.

Joe Flower, "Why 'Free Market Competition' Fails in Health Care," Imagine What If, November 2, 2009. www.imaginewhatif.com. Used by permission of the author.

As you read, consider the following questions:

1. What does Flower mean when he writes, "Aggregate risk varies by socioeconomic class and age"?
2. According to Flower, why is the difficult distinction between absolute demand and optional demand a stumbling block to free-market health care?
3. Why are peer-reviewed literature and other checks on medical judgment crucial to doctor-patient trust, as Flower suggests?

In trying to think about the future of health care, thoughtful, intelligent people often ask, "Why can't we just let the free market operate in health care? That would drive down costs and drive up quality." They point to the successes of competition in other industries. But their faith is misplaced [because of] economic reasons that are peculiar to health care.

Three Reasons Free-Market Principles Will Not Work

More "free market" competition could definitely improve the future of health care in certain areas. But the problems of the sector as a whole will not yield to "free market" ideas—never will, never can—for reasons that are ineluctable, that derive from the core nature of the market. We might parse them out into three:

1. *True medical demand is wildly variable, random, and absolute.* Some people get cancer, others don't. Some keel over from a heart attack, get shot, or fall off a cliff—others are in and out of hospitals for years before they die.

Aggregate risk varies by socioeconomic class and age—the older you are, the more likely you are to need medical attention; poor and uneducated people are more likely to get diabetes. Individual risk varies somewhat by lifestyle—people who eat better and exercise have lower risk of some diseases; people who sky dive, ski, or hang out in certain bars have higher risk of trauma.

But crucially, risk has no relation to ability to pay. A poor person does not suddenly discover an absolute need to buy a new Jaguar, but may well suddenly discover an absolute need for the services of a neurosurgeon, an oncologist, a cancer center, and everything that goes with it. And the need is truly absolute. The demand is literally, "You obtain this or you die."

2. *All demand apes this absolute demand.* Medicine is a matter of high skill and enormous knowledge. So doctors, by necessity, act as sellers, and agents of other sellers (hospitals, labs, pharmaceutical companies). Buyers must depend on the judgment of sellers as to what is necessary, or even prudent. The phrase "Doctor's orders" has a peremptory and absolute flavor.

For the most part, people do not access health care for fun. Recreational colonoscopies are not big drivers of health care costs. In some cases, such as cosmetic surgery or laser eye corrections, the decision is clearly one the buyer can make. It's a classic economic decision: "Do I like this enough to pay for it?" But for the most part, people only access health care because they feel they have to. And in most situations, it is difficult for the buyer to differentiate the truly absolute demand ("Do this or you die") from the optional.

Often it is difficult even for the doctor to tell the difference. The doctor may be able truthfully to say, "Get this mitral valve replaced or you will die. Soon." More often, it's a judgment call, a matter of probabilities, and a matter of quality of life: "You will likely live longer, and suffer less, if you get a new mitral valve, get a new hip, take this statin."

At the same time the doctor, operating both as seller and effectively as agent for the buyer, is often rewarded for selling more (directly through fees and indirectly through ownership of labs and other services), and is not only not rewarded, but actually punished, for doing less (through the loss of business, the threat of malpractice suits, and punishment for insufficiently justifying coding).

So the seller is agent for the buyer, the seller is rewarded for doing more and punished for doing less, and neither the buyer nor the seller can easily tell the difference between what is really necessary and what is optional.

This is especially true because the consequences of the decision are so often separated from the decision. "Eat your broccoli" may actually be a life-or-death demand; maybe you need to eat more vegetables to avoid a heart attack. But you're not going to die tonight because you pushed the broccoli around the plate and then hid it under the bread.

So, because it is complex and difficult, and because its consequences are often not immediate and obvious, the buy decision is effectively transferred to the seller. We depend on the seller (the doctor) to tell us what we need. Whether we buy or not usually depends almost solely on whether we trust the doctor and believe what the doctor says.

3. *The benefit of medical capacity accrues even to those who do not use it.* Imagine a society with no police. Having police benefits you even if you never are the victim of a crime. You benefit from that new bridge even if you never drive over it, because it eases the traffic jams on the roads you do travel, because your customers and employees and co-workers use it, and because development in the whole region benefits from the new bridge.

This is the infrastructure argument. Every part of health care, from ambulances and emergency room capacity to public health education to mass vaccinations to cutting-edge medical research, benefits the society as a whole, even those who do not use that particular piece. This is true even of those who do not realize that they benefit from it, even of those who deny that they benefit from it. They benefit from having a healthier work force, from keeping epidemics in check, from the increased development that accrues to a region that has good medical capacity—even from the reduction in medical costs brought about by some medical spending, as when a good diabetes program keeps people from having to use the Emergency Room.

Market Forces Cannot Help Those Who Need Medical Attention Now

In the case of free market innovations in consumer goods . . . prices tend to drop over time. . . .

Were we to take a pure, free-market approach, it is reasonable to expect that accessibility to the CT scanner that can discover your cancer will cost less a few years after introduction into the market. But . . . somebody who has cancer now can't wait those couple of years to gain access. By the time they can afford the test, they could well be dead or have a disease so advanced they soon will be.

Rick Ungar, "Can a Free Market Economy
Deliver Affordable Healthcare to All? Don't Bet
on It," True/Slant, February 27, 2010.
http://trueslant.com.

All three of these core factors show why health care is not responsive to classic economic supply-and-demand theory, and why the "free market" is not a satisfactory economic model for health care, even if you are otherwise a believer in it.

Spreading Costs to Everyone in Society

The answer to the first problem, the variability and absolute nature of risk, is clearly to spread the risk over all who share it, even if it is invisible to them. If you drive a car, you must have car insurance, and your gas taxes contribute to maintaining the infrastructure of roads and bridges; if you own a home, you must have fire insurance, and your property taxes pay for the fire department. Because of your ownership and use of these things, you not only must insure yourself against loss, you also must pay part of the infrastructure costs that your use of them occasions. Similarly, all owners and operators of human bodies need to insure against problems that may accrue to their own body, and pay some of the infrastructure costs that their use of that body occasions. However the insurance is structured and paid for, somehow everyone who has a body needs to be insured for it—the cost of the risk must be spread across the population.

Skipping to the third problem, the infrastructure argument, its answer is somewhat similar: To the extent to which health care capacity is infrastructure, like police, fire, ports, highways, and public education, the costs are properly assigned to the society as a whole; they are the type of costs that we normally assign to government, and pay for through taxes, rather than per transaction. In every developed country, including the United States, health care gets large subsidies from government, because it is seen as an infrastructure capacity.

The Need for Evidence-Based Accountability

That leaves the second problem, the way in which all demand apes the absolute nature of true demand in health care ("Get this or die"). The answer to this problem is more nuanced, because it is not possible to stop depending on the judgment of physicians. Medical judgment is, in the end, why we have doctors at all. But we can demand that doctors apply not just their own judgment in the moment, but the research and judgment of their profession. This is the argument for evidence-based medicine and comparative effectiveness research. If a knee surgeon wishes to argue that you should have your arthritic knee replaced when, according to the judgment of the profession as a whole, the better answer in your situation is a cortisone shot and gentle daily yoga, the surgeon should have to justify somehow, even if just for the record, why your case is different and special. The physician's capacity to make a buy decision on your behalf must be restrained at least by the profession's medical judgment. If the best minds in the profession, publishing in the peer-reviewed literature, have come to the conclusion that a particular procedure is ineffective, unwarranted, or even dangerous, it is reasonable for insurers, public or private, to follow that best medical judgment and stop paying for it.

The Health Care System Is Too Complex and Nuanced

These three core factors—the absolute and variable nature of health care demand, the complexity of medicine, and the infrastructure-like nature of health care capacity—are all endemic to health care and cannot be separated from it. And all three dictate that health care cannot work as a classic economic response to market demands. Failure to acknowledge these three core factors and structure health care payments around them account for much of the current market's inability to deliver value. Paying "fee for service," when the doctor is both the seller and acting as agent for the buyer, and when the doctor is punished for doing less, is a prescription for always doing more, whether "more" delivers more value or not. Paying "fee for service," unrestrained by any way to make classic value judgments, means that hospitals and medical centers respond to competition by adding capacity and offering more services, whether or not those services are really needed or add value.

For all these reasons, it is vastly more complex to structure a health care market rationally, in a way that delivers real value, than it is to structure any other sector, and simply fostering "free market" competition will not solve the problem.

> *"Year in and year out ... analysis has shown consistently that CDH [consumer-driven health] plans save money on a sustained basis for employers and employees, regardless of the health of the individual and without compromising care."*

Consumer-Driven Health Care Is More Affordable

William J. Reindl

Consumer-driven health care (CDH) plans arose in the 1990s as an alternative to more traditional insurance in which individuals lose a significant portion of their wages to pay for insurance they may or may not use. Those who opt for CDH plans typically pay a smaller part of their wages into a Health Savings Account (HSA) that acts as resource fund from which to pay for routine health care costs. The insured individuals also receive cheaper catastrophic insurance coverage with a high deductible to protect against severe injury or illness. In the following viewpoint, William J. Reindl claims that CDH plans have proven successful at reducing overall patient health care costs while allowing consumers to keep more of their income. He also insists that even though HSAs provide limited funds for health care, studies have shown that consumers

William J. Reindl, "Mythbusters: The Facts Are in About Consumer-Driven Health Care," *Benefits Quarterly*, vol. 26, no. 1, First Quarter 2010, p. 4. Used by permission of the International Society of Certified Employee Benefits Specialists.

do not forgo needed services or routine checkups to conserve these dollars. In Reindl's view, CDH plans need to remain a vital part of health care reform aimed at lowering costs while providing needed care. William J. Reindl is a senior vice president at CIGNA health insurance who has shaped that company's consumer-driven health care offerings.

As you read, consider the following questions:

1. According to a 2009 survey of CIGNA insurance purchasers cited by Reindl, how much less was the medical spending of CDH consumers with diabetes than their counterparts in other plans?
2. Pharmacy costs were typically decreased by what percent for consumers newly enrolled in CIGNA CDH plans as compared to other plans, according to the CIGNA survey Reindl references?
3. What is a benefit-neutral CDH plan, as Reindl describes it?

This fall [of 2010] America is engaged in a debate to determine the future of health care and the role of health insurance.

Lost in the middle of this debate are consumer-driven health (CDH) plans. During the past several years, CDH plans have demonstrated they can help create a more affordable, sustainable, high-quality—and healthier—health care system.

Yet many continue not to see the value of CDH plans through the fog of misperceptions such as: "CDH plans don't reduce costs, they merely shift them," "These plans are only for the youngest, healthiest and richest"—and worst of all—"CDH plans are forcing individuals to forgo needed care."

These misperceptions have led some to the equally wrongheaded conclusion: "With national health care reform, CDH plans will become unnecessary."

As the United States debates the future of health care and health insurance, it is vitally important to dispel the fog of misinformation and examine the facts.

CDH Plans Save Money

During the past four years, CIGNA has analyzed and compared the actual claims paid by a total of one million people covered by its CDH and traditional preferred provider organization (PPO) and health maintenance organization (HMO) plans.

Year in and year out, this analysis has shown consistently that CDH plans save money on a sustained basis for employers and employees, regardless of the health of the individual and without compromising care.

CIGNA's most recent study, released in January 2009, compiled and analyzed two years' worth of health care claims experience of 440,000 people enrolled in CIGNA CDH and traditional HMO and PPO plans. It exploded the common myths about CDH plans.

The first myth is that a CDH plan does not reduce costs but rather shifts them, and cost savings are not sustained. CIGNA found that in the first year, normalized medical trend for CIGNA CDH plans was −3.3% vs. 10.6% for traditional plans—almost a 14% difference, as shown in Figure 1. Again, this analysis compares individuals that are in different types of CIGNA plans with the same employer. The study also showed that lower medical trend for CDH plans continues in subsequent years.

CDH Plans Are Not Just for the Young and Healthy

Similarly, the study debunked a second common myth that CDH plans "cherry pick" the youngest, healthiest and richest while forcing managed care plans to charge more to cover the sickest patients.

The data show that CDH enrollment covers the spectrum of healthy to chronically ill. CIGNA observed CDH plan savings for all health status categories, with greater savings for less healthy individuals.

Notably, CIGNA looked specifically at the experience of those with two common chronic conditions: hypertension or diabetes. As shown in Figure 2, of the 22,000 individuals in the study that have either hypertension or diabetes, the medical cost trend was substantially less for CIGNA CDH plan customers with diabetes (20% less) or hypertension (18% less) than for individuals with either of those diseases in traditional CIGNA health plans.

Moreover, these individuals maintained similar treatment regimens regardless of whether they were covered by CDH, HMO or PPO plans, suggesting that the lower cost trend is a result of better chronic disease management, rather than patients forgoing recommended care.

CDH Insured Do Not Skimp on Care

The third key myth is that CDH plans are causing individuals to forgo needed care. CIGNA's data effectively dispel this allegation with multiple years of evidence consistently showing that those in CDH plans receive the same or better care than their counterparts covered in PPO and HMO plans.

For a fourth year in a row, the study showed those in CDH plans continued to receive recommended care at the same or higher levels as those enrolled in traditional plans in an evaluation of compliance with more than 300 evidence-based measures of health care quality (for example, women having a mammogram in the past 24 months or diabetes patients having a physician visit in the last six months).

Notably, using nationally recommended evidence-based standards of care—the care measures proven to work best—improves costs. These cost savings amount to approximately $355 per person insured per year, including $149 in direct medical costs and $206 in indirect productivity savings.

Not only does the data show that CDH plans save money without compromising care, but there is mounting evidence that

Figure 1: Projected Medical Costs per $100 Spent CIGNA Choice Fund vs. Traditional Plans

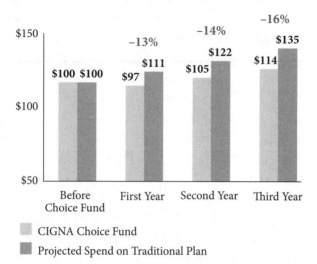

CIGNA Choice Fund

Projected Spend on Traditional Plan

Analysis excluded catastrophic claims >$50,000 and capitated services.

Figure 2: Medical Cost Trend Reduction Compared to Traditional Plans

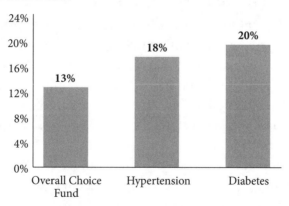

Results are normalized for their risk scores, and catastrophic claims exceeding $50,000 are excluded.

TAKEN FROM: William J. Reindl, "Mythbusters: The Facts Are in About Consumer-Driven Health Plans," *Benefits Quarterly*, First Quarter, 2010.

suggests people in these programs are increasingly engaged and smarter about their health care.

For example, the study shows that those covered in CDH plans were more likely to utilize preventive services—such as annual checkups, and breast and colon cancer screenings.

First-year preventive care utilization was 8% greater among those in CDH plans compared to traditional plans, and second-year CIGNA CDH plan preventive care utilization was 15% greater when compared to traditional plans.

Compliance and cost savings were also evident in the pharmacy component of CDH plans.... Pharmacy cost trend for those newly enrolled in CIGNA CDH plans was 10% less than for those enrolled in traditional plans. When compared with the prior year, usage was higher for new CIGNA CDH plan individuals and average unit cost trend was less for maintenance medications, suggesting that these individuals were compliant with medications while exercising lower-cost options such as purchasing medications by mail order and electing to use generic medications. . . .

Services Tailored to Consumer's Needs

A key element of CDH plan design that has been demonstrated to reduce costs without compromising care is to offer a *benefit-neutral* plan—one that offers benefit levels that are comparable to previous traditional plans. For example, if a traditional PPO has a $500 deductible, an employer can offer a CDH with a $1,500 deductible offset with a $1,000 health savings or health reimbursement account.

This approach has been proven to reduce costs year over year without shifting costs to individuals and offers true value to prospective enrollees.

Another key component for a successful CDH plan is online decision support tools that enable individuals to determine the best sources of quality health care at the appropriate price.

Just a few years ago, medical cost and quality information was entirely opaque. Today, individuals can look online to see an entire episode of care for their illness or injury, starting with qualified medical information about their illness and treatment options, probabilities of certain treatments, listings of the best local doctors and hospitals specializing in the specific treatments, cost ranges by specialist or facility, and even cost comparisons of medications.

CIGNA's own experience is that those enrolled in CDH plans are nearly twice as likely to register to use myCIGNA.com's online health care quality, cost and health improvement resources.

Provided with quality and cost information, individuals may identify specialists and hospitals qualifying for the CIGNA Care Network, a performance-based program for health care professionals that meet CIGNA and third-party quality measures. This program maximizes cost savings while maintaining high quality. On average, those who select CIGNA Care Network health care professionals may experience:

- 34% fewer hospital deaths
- 39% fewer hospital complications
- 47% lower hospital costs.

By using CIGNA's quality and cost information to choose a specialist, they experience:

- 4% to 5% improvement in clinical quality indicators
- 29% reduction in hospital readmissions
- 8% to 12% lower total medical costs.

Well-designed CDH plans provide 100% coverage of preventive health services, including routine checkups, breast and colon cancer screenings, critical diabetic care and child immunizations. Not only can these services be critical for early detection of potential health issues, they have shown to improve the individual's overall health and plan satisfaction.

Similarly, effective CDH plans feature health coaching, providing telephone outreach from specially trained health advisors that help individuals navigate the health care system, understand how their lifestyle choices can affect their overall health, and access information about cost and quality. This program includes outreach to individuals whose health risk assessment indicates that they may be at risk.

When these design features are present and effectively communicated, individuals are more likely to enroll in these plans. . . .

CIGNA's annual studies of claims experience have consistently shown that customers switching to CDH plans achieve double-digit percentage reductions in total medical cost trend, without sacrificing care. And the cost savings continue in subsequent years.

There is also mounting evidence that people in CDH plans are more engaged and smarter about managing their health, and in fact have demanded cost and quality transparency information so that they can be better managers of their own health and health finances. CDH plans will continue to spawn this type of value-oriented behavior and subsequent innovation, which is key to long-term cost reduction and quality improvement.

If health care reform goals are to be achieved, well-designed CDH plans—those that are benefit-neutral to the individual and reduce costs, not shift costs—should play a significant role.

> *"Insistence on greater consumer participation in the form of co-payments at the point of service will lead to rationing effects on both necessary and unnecessary health services."*

Consumer-Driven Health Care Is Less Effective

Carol L. Owen

In the following viewpoint, Carol L. Owen calls upon fellow social workers to rally behind universal health care in the United States. In her argument, Owen recounts the advent of consumer-driven health care plans in the 1990s as a potential method of reigning in health care costs. Owen points to studies that have concluded that consumer-driven plans encourage consumers to ration their health care for fear of paying high deductibles and depleting funds accrued in their health savings accounts (HSAs). Owen maintains consumer-driven plans are only beneficial to wealthy purchasers who use the plans as a tax shelter. She believes these plans are less efficient for poor Americans or those who have chronic illnesses that require a lot of monthly expenditures. For these reasons, Owen advocates that social workers oppose attempts to increase consumer-driven health care at the expense of universal coverage.

Carol L. Owen, "Consumer-Driven Health Care: Answer to Global Competition or Threat to Social Justice?" *Social Work*, vol. 54, no. 4, October 2009. Copyrighted material reprinted with permission from the National Association of Social Workers, Inc.

Carol L. Owen is a professor in the Department of Health and Human Services at Salem State College in Massachusetts.

As you read, consider the following questions:
1. Why does Owen claim that HSAs are not appropriate to low- and moderate-income consumers?
2. According to Owen, the failure of what plan in the 1990s led to the rise of HSAs and other consumer-driven plans?
3. As Owen asserts, a preferable alternative to consumer-driven health care would be the reinvention of what kind of "risk pooling"?

Philosophically, many advocates of consumer-driven health care believe that health care costs are out of control because most Americans are too generously insured. They argue that removing controls that currently limit consumer choices of providers and services will result in competition and innovations that will improve overall value. Proponents of HSAs [health savings accounts] call for increasing patient sensitivity to cost and quality issues by having them spend more of their own money on health care. Under this line of reasoning, Americans are seen as likely to make health care purchasing decisions as they make other economic decisions—that is, on the basis of their personal preferences for certain goods and services, in combination with their ideas about the quality of the goods and services they seek to purchase.

Conservative think tanks such as the CATO Institute, the Galen Institute, the Heritage Foundation, and the American Enterprise Institute have allied under a health policy-focused umbrella called the Health Policy Consensus Group. Its purpose is to maximize the group's collective voice in restraining the role of the federal government in health care reform, in advocating the transfer of health policymaking back to the states, and in supporting President [George W.] Bush's earlier efforts to avoid new taxes that might be needed to expand programs such as the State Children's Insurance Program. Consensus group partners draw on an economic construct referred to as "crowd out" to describe effects of expansion of governmentally sponsored health programs on the private health insurance market. Liberal critics claim just the opposite: that the nation's attachment to employer-based and commercially sponsored health insurance actually crowds out political will to solve the appalling national problem of lack of insurance for approximately 46 million U.S. citizens.

Cost Sharing Can Lead to Skimping on Health Care

Evidence has long suggested that insistence on greater consumer participation in the form of co-payments at the point of service will lead to rationing effects on both necessary and unnecessary health services. Recent analyses of a classic RAND Corporation experimental design study conducted in 1982 have concluded further that cost sharing at the time of service fails to encourage consumers to take better care of themselves or to either seek or experience higher quality care. A meta-study of 132 articles examining the relationship between cost sharing and service delivery concluded that higher copayments charged at time of service are associated not only with self-rationing of medical appointments, but also with poorer compliance with medical advice in the form of decreased use of recommended medications and discontinuation of therapies. Researchers who study the effects of cost sharing between insurers and consumers have emphasized that the share arrangement should be structured in ways that do not interfere with patients showing up for critical services at the time they most urgently need help.

The most obvious risks associated with HSAs and other consumer-driven approaches apply to individuals with compromised health status or limited income. The largest advantages of HSAs accrue to consumers in the highest tax brackets, because contributions to these accounts operate as tax shields.

Consumers in the lowest tax brackets are more likely to experience daily challenges in meeting their basic household expenses. Low- and moderate-income consumers are more likely to lack the discretionary income to contribute to an HSA. In addition, being subject to a lower tax rate means a substantially smaller tax break than that experienced by wealthier taxpayers. A [2005] Commonwealth Fund task force concluded that "health savings accounts are not likely to be an important contributor to expanding coverage among uninsured people because most of them do not face high-enough marginal tax rates to benefit substantially from the tax deductibility of the HSA contributions." Further support for this conclusion is contained in data from *Current Population Survey* (CPS), which reveals that approximately 55 percent of uninsured Americans are in the 0 percent tax bracket, and an additional 16 percent of uninsureds are in the 10 percent tax bracket.

Another issue of concern relates to individuals who live with chronic health conditions. People with chronic health conditions typically make more frequent visits each year to their doctors than do patients with acute illnesses or injuries. An HSA that is structured with a high deductible may function as a continuous drain on the financial resources of a person with a chronic illness such as diabetes, heart disease, multiple sclerosis, or cancer. This would make it difficult for that individual to replenish savings to meet the following year's high deductible, co-payments, and other out-of-pocket health care expenses. . . .

Circumstances Leading to Consumer-Driven Models

By the 1950s, employer-sponsored health insurance was the norm. This arrangement saw employers paying most of the cost of the insurance premiums, in return for a business tax deduction. Earlier, the hospital industry had pioneered its own insurance plan during the Great Depression under the name Blue Cross. Blue Cross insurance plans helped middle-class families to defray hospital expenses that otherwise might have led to personal bankruptcies. Blue Cross was soon joined by Blue Shield, an invention of the medical community that was designed to assist those who needed assistance with paying their physicians' fees. "The Blues," as these private plans were jointly called, were incorporated as nonprofit entities. The plans were sold through community groups and also through many U.S. corporations. The Blue Cross plan alone reported enrollment of 6 million people by the time the U.S. entered World War II. This huge enrollment changed the face of health care payment and solidified the trend toward employer-sponsored insurance.

Pressures for cost containment followed the 1965 passage of Medicare and Medicaid, the public insurance programs initiated under President Lyndon Johnson's administration that offered coverage to elderly people, people with disabilities, and low-income children and families who had been left out of private insurance plans. With more Americans covered by either public or private insurance, greater use of health services became a pattern that invited a new paradigm of "managed care" to monitor costs, utilization, and quality. Insurance companies adopted "selective contracting," or signing up only a fraction of health care providers in given communities. Utilization review panels looked over service usage patterns in physicians' offices and hospitals to ensure that only the most "medically necessary" services were delivered.

Yet despite intensified cost-containment measures introduced by government and private managed care companies, inflation in health care costs continued to spiral. [In the book *Health and Mental Health Policy: A Biopsychosocial Perspective*, Cynthia Moniz and Stephen Gorin write] "By 1990, health care expenditures equaled 12.1 percent of GDP [gross domestic product], up from 8.9 percent in 1980." At the same time, the number of people without health insurance had grown to 33.4 million, and "tens of millions more had limited or inadequate insurance."

During Bill Clinton's 1991 campaign for the presidency, a plan called "managed competition" was advocated by health economist Alan Enthoven, physician Paul Ellwood, and others. The idea was to encourage stiff competition for subscribers among managed care organizations on the basis of cost and quality statistics that would be publicized. The vision advanced by proponents of managed competition was of an entire nation of subscribers enrolled in managed care plans. When Clinton won the presidency, he promised health care reform that sounded like it would offer universal coverage through an employer mandate. Costs would be further restrained by allowing purchasing alliances and by involving the government in the determination of a national health budget. Though organized labor was largely in favor of Clinton's Health Security Act, many insurance companies stood to lose ground in the health market and actively lobbied against its passage. Their argument was a familiar one: You don't want the government involved in determining your health care choices. "Social workers were also ambivalent about the act" [Moniz and Gorin claim]. While noting that some of its features were consonant with the preferences of the profession for passage of a single-payer system, social work withheld official support.

Despite the failure of Clinton's health proposal to win a majority in Congress, various aspects of managed competition began to permeate the health care field. Health care provider "report cards" based on quality and cost measures were publicized by insurance companies. Patients were encouraged to use these report cards to select their doctors, hospitals, and laboratories. The stage was set for creation of a consumer-driven or consumer-directed health care system in which marketwise health care consumers were predicted to moderate overall costs in the U.S. health care system by using self-restraint in their individual health service purchasing decisions. Computer technologies were increasingly claimed to improve efficiency, as Internet-disseminated provider report cards made more transparent the cost and quality profiles of the rated physicians and hospitals. Although the outcome data are quite mixed regarding the effectiveness of managed competition in restraining costs, many recent health policy proposals continue to build on the 1980s and 1990s reforms just described. . . .

Universal Health Care Is the Better Choice

At the turn of the 21st century, there have been efforts to align the ethical construct of social justice with human rights. This merged discourse implies that all human beings have inherent dignity and worth and should be guaranteed certain basic rights and materials that are necessary to meet their basic human needs. Social workers have increasingly adopted this perspective and are joining the ranks of activists who cite specific human rights principles described in the *Universal Declaration of Human Rights* as a fulcrum for advocating universal access to health care, decent housing, and public elementary education, as well as ensuring other basic protections.

Social work has begun to enter coalitions with other professional and advocacy groups that ground their demands for the creation of a universal health care system in human rights principles. In alliance with the American Academy of Family Physicians, the American Academy of Pediatrics, the American Nurses Association, the American Hospital Association, the American Geriatrics Society, and numerous other professional societies, NASW [National Association of Social Workers] subscribes to health care reforms that are inclusive of all citizens. By joining Divided We Fail, a coalition with sufficient breadth to include the Service Employees International Union, the American Association of Retired Persons, and the Business Roundtable, professional social work has affirmed its commitment to universality in insurance coverage. Strength for the position of health care as a human right is found in the *Universal Declaration of Human Rights*, a consensual agreement signed in 1948 by the United States and 50 other nations, which asserts a right for each person to a standard of living adequate for the health and wellbeing of himself [or herself], including food, clothing, housing and medical care and necessary social services, and the right of security in the event of unemployment, sickness, disability, widowhood, old age or other lack of livelihood in circumstances beyond his [or her] control. . . .

Moving Toward Equitable Health Care

Health care reforms of the market-based or consumer-driven variety are antagonistic with efforts to align U.S. health policy more closely with the human rights principles articulated in the *Universal Declaration of Human Rights*. HSAs and related structural reforms that require a larger financial commitment by consumers in return for individual tax deductions have the potential to punish societal members with the greatest health care needs and most compromised incomes while rewarding those members who are healthy and enjoy higher incomes. An alternative to the market reforms currently being advanced under the name of "consumer-driven health care" is the reinvention of community pooling solutions that align sick and well members within a defined community or work setting to share financial risk. As the United States' 60-year-old employer-sponsored health insurance system sinks farther and farther toward financial unmanageability, a reinvention of community risk pooling will require strong backing by the government.

Social workers are ideally positioned, because of a strong ethical and political history, as well as affinity with disadvantaged clients, to play a role in the current health policy discourse. This discourse will decide which policy fork in the road the United States will take: toward more market competition and consumer responsibility, or toward a partnership of public and private sectors to guarantee certain basic protections for all citizens.

Periodical Bibliography

The following articles have been selected to supplement the diverse views presented in this chapter.

Christine Bechtel and Debra L. Ness	"If You Build It, Will They Come? Designing Truly Patient-Centered Health Care," *Health Affairs*, May 2010.
Ronald Brownstein	"First, Do No Harm," *National Journal*, April 16, 2011.
Roger Bybee	"Can We Have Universal Health Care?" *Dissent*, Spring 2009.
Philip Klein	"The Matter with Myths," *American Spectator*, July/August 2009.
Kathy Klug and Lois Chianese	"Health Savings Accounts: Back to the Future," *Benefits Quarterly*, First Quarter 2010.
Frank W. Maletz	"From Hospital to 'Healthspital,'" *Futurist*, March/April 2011.
Paul Menzel and Donald W. Light	"A Conservative Case for Universal Access to Health Care," *Hastings Center Report*, July/August 2006.
Carol L. Owen	"Consumer-Driven Health Care: Answer to Global Competition or Threat to Social Justice," *Social Work*, October 2009.
T.R. Reid	"No Country for Sick Men," *Newsweek*, September 21, 2009.
D. Eric Schansberg	"Envisioning a Free Market in Health Care," *CATO Journal*, Winter 2011.
James H. Stephens and Gerald R. Ledlow	"Real Healthcare Reform: Focus on Primary Care Access," *Hospital Topics*, vol. 88, no. 4, 2010.

CHAPTER 4

How Will the 2010 Health Care Reform Law Impact America?

Chapter Preface

The 2010 health care reform legislation provides the most sweeping changes to the US health care system since the Social Security Act of 1965. That year Medicare and Medicaid were created, providing health care to the nation's elderly and disabled and to low-income individuals. Today the new health care legislation opens the doors to a variety of services that some have argued are as significant as Medicare and Medicaid.

The Patient Protection and Affordable Care Act (PPACA) is the heart of this legislation, comprising a series of entitlements that will continue to develop through 2020. Some of the more notable legislation includes: allowing children to stay on their parents' health insurance until the age of 26 (effective September 23, 2010); preventing insurers from discriminating against or charging higher rates to people with pre-existing medical conditions (effective January 1, 2014); and expanding Medicaid benefits for people with income up to 133% of the poverty line, including adults without dependents (effective January 1, 2014).

Another benefit provides financial relief to people on Medicare for expensive prescription drugs. In 2010 Don Berwick, administrator of the Centers for Medicare and Medicaid Services, confirmed that 1 million rebate checks at $250 a piece were sent out to help recipients close the gap between what Medicare pays for drugs and the remaining balance consumers pay. This "donut hole" will continue to shrink in 2011 when individuals will "receive a 50 percent discount when buying covered brand-name prescription drugs," Berwick posted on the White House blog on August 30, 2010.

The PPACA also provides tools to help curb unreasonable price hikes in insurance premiums. According to Jay Angoff, director of the Office of Consumer Information and Insurance Oversight, insurers will now be required to have their proposed rate increases go through state scrutiny before they reach the customer. This process, known as rate review, is a part of the nation's new $250 million initiative toward consumer protection.

Former Secretary of Commerce Gary Locke announced on August 31, 2010, that employers, too, will benefit from this health care reform legislation. According to his statement on HealthCare.gov, the Early Retiree Reinsurance Program is one example of a PPACA program that assists employers who want to take care of their older employees. The law permits employers to apply for eligibility in a $5 billion program designed to help them aid retiring employees who are over 55 but are not yet eligible for Medicare. As of the date of Locke's announcement, nearly 2,000 employers and unions were successfully participating in the program, helping "their employees make this transition comfortably and [providing them with] access to health insurance past retirement."

To subsidize these benefits, revenues will have to come from citizens. The source will not be through taxes, but through mandatory purchasing of health insurance, also known as the individual mandate. There is a common element between taxation and the individual mandate: the IRS, which will serve as the enforcer of these purchases. Starting in 2014, if an individual has not bought health insurance, penalties will include a $695 fine or 2.5% of their income, whichever is higher. By 2016 penalties could increase to $1,000. As of May 2011, the constitutionality of the individual mandate was being challenged in more than thirty states. In December 2010 District Judge Henry Hudson of Virginia struck down the law, claiming it "exceeds the constitutional boundaries of congressional power." In the following chapter, opponents of the PPACA support Hudson's opinion, arguing the law is unjust and unconstitutional. Their views are countered in the chapter by advocates who believe that, if given a chance, the PPACA will help rein in skyrocketing costs as well as provide more adequate insurance for millions of Americans.

"These reforms give you more control over your health care."

Health Care Reform Law Expands Coverage to Millions of Americans

Barack Obama

On March 23, 2010, after signing the Patient Protection and Affordable Care Act (PPACA) into effect, Barack Obama, the forty-fourth president of the United States, gave the speech encapsulated in the following viewpoint. Obama claims that the act will not compel Americans to change their health insurance plans if they are satisfied with their coverage; however, the president believes new measures will expand coverage to more uninsured Americans by removing some current barriers and by the creation of a health insurance exchange that will create larger pools of consumers and thus spread risk and lower premiums. Obama also asserts that new tax breaks to small businesses will allow those companies who could not previously afford to cover their employees to inaugurate health benefits. The president claims the advantages of the PPACA will become apparent soon, convincing even the skeptics that the new model will serve the nation well.

Barack Obama, "Remarks on the Patient Protection and Affordable Care Act," *Daily Compilation of Presidential Documents*, March 23, 2010.

As you read, consider the following questions:

1. Why does Obama claim the PPACA is not a "government takeover"?
2. Under the PPACA, until what age can children stay enrolled on their parents' health plan, according to the president?
3. As the president argues, what political party came up with the concept of the health insurance exchange?

After a century of striving, after a year of debate, after a historic vote, health care reform is no longer an unmet promise, it is the law of the land. It is the law of the land.

And although it may be my signature that's affixed to the bottom of this bill, it was your work, your commitment, your unyielding hope that made this victory possible. When the special interests deployed an army of lobbyists, an onslaught of negative ads to preserve the status quo, you didn't give up. You hit the phones, and you took to the streets. You mobilized, and you organized. You turned up the pressure, and you kept up the fight.

When the pundits were obsessing over who was up and who was down, you never lost sight of what was right and what was wrong. You knew this wasn't about the fortunes of a party; this was about the future of our country. And when the opposition said this just wasn't the right time, you didn't want to wait another year or another decade or another generation for reform. You felt the fierce urgency of now.

You met the lies with truth. You met cynicism with conviction. Most of all, you met fear with a force that's a lot more powerful, and that is faith in America. You met it with hope.

A Victory for All Americans

Despite decades in which Washington failed to tackle our toughest challenges, despite the smallness of so much of what passes for politics these days, despite those who said that progress was impossible, you made people believe that people who love this country can still change it. So this victory is not mine; it is your victory. It's a victory for the United States of America.

For 2 years on the campaign trail, and for the past year as we've worked to reform our system of health insurance, it's been folks like you who have propelled this movement and kept us fixed on what was at stake in this fight. And rarely has a day gone by that I haven't heard from somebody personally—whether in a letter, or an e-mail, or at a town hall—who's reminded me of why it was so important that we not give up, who reminded me why we could not quit.

I heard from Ryan Smith, who's here today, and runs a small business with five employees. He is trying to do the right thing, paying for half of the cost of coverage for his workers. But as his premiums keep on going up and up and up, he's worried he's going to have to stop offering health care for his people. But because of this bill, he is now going to be getting tax credits that allow him to do what he knows is the right thing to do, and that's going to be true for millions of employers all across America.

I heard the story of 11-year-old Marcelas Owens, who's right here, looking sharp. . . . He and I made sure to coordinate our ties today. Yes, it looks good.

Marcelas is a wonderful young man, and he lost his mom to illness. And she didn't have insurance and couldn't afford the care that she needed. So in her memory, Marcelas, 11 years old, has told her story across America so that no other children have to go through what his family has experienced. That's why we don't quit.

I heard from folks like Natoma Canfield, who had to give up her health coverage after her rates were jacked up by more than 40 percent. And she was terrified that an illness would mean she'd lose the house that her parent built, but she also knew that if she was burdened by these huge premiums, that she wouldn't be able to pay the mortgage. So she finally decided not to keep her health insurance. And she's now lying in a hospital bed, as we speak, faced with just such an illness, and she's praying that she can somehow afford to get well. And her sister Connie is here today. And it's because of Natoma's family that we could not quit.

I've met people like Ashley Baia, who worked for my campaign. Where's Ashley? She's around here somewhere, I know she is. There she is, right in front. She just doesn't like waving. Ashley decided to get involved with our campaign a couple of years ago because her own mother lost her job and with it her health insurance when she got sick. And they had to file bankruptcy. And so Ashley worked tirelessly, not to get me elected, but to solve a problem that millions of families across the country were facing.

Each of these Americans made their voices heard. And it's because of them, so many others, so many of you, that real, meaningful change is coming to the United States of America. It is because of you that we did not quit. It's because of you that Congress did not quit. It's because of you that I did not quit. It's because of you.

No Government Takeover

Now, let me tell you what change looks like, because those fighting change are still out there, still making a lot of noise about what this reform means. So I want the American people to understand it and look it up for yourself. Go on our web site, whitehouse.gov, or go to any credible news outlet's web site and look in terms of what reform will mean for you.

I said this once or twice, but it bears repeating: If you like your current insurance, you will keep your current insurance. No Government takeover; nobody is changing what you've got if you're happy with it. If you like your doctor, you will be able to keep your doctor. In fact, more people will keep their doctors because your coverage will be more secure and more stable than it was before I signed this legislation.

And now that this legislation is passed, you don't have to take my word for it. You'll be able to see it in your own lives. I heard one of the Republican leaders say this was going to be

Armageddon. Well, 2 months from now, 6 months from now, you can check it out. We'll look around and we'll see. You don't have to take my word for it.

So what works in our system won't change. And a lot of people are happy with the health care that they've got, and that won't change because of this legislation. Here's what will change, and here's what will change right away.

Tax Breaks for Small Businesses and No Barriers to Coverage

This year, we'll start offering tax credits to about 4 million small businesses to help them cover the cost of coverage. And that means that folks like Ryan will immediately get a tax break so that he can better afford the coverage he's already providing for his employees. And who knows, because of that tax break, he may decide to hire a couple more folks in his small business, because of this legislation.

This year, tens of thousands of uninsured Americans with a preexisting condition and parents whose children have a pre-existing condition will finally be able to purchase the coverage they need. And that means folks like Natoma Canfield will have access to affordable insurance. That happens this year.

This year, insurance companies will no longer be able to drop people's coverage when they get sick, or place lifetime limits or restrictive annual limits on the amount of care they can receive. This year, all new insurance plans will be required to offer free preventive care. And this year, young adults will be able to stay on their parents' policies until they're 26 years old. That all happens this year.

This year, seniors who fall in the coverage gap known as the doughnut hole will get some help to help pay for prescription drugs. And I want seniors to know, despite what some have said, these reforms will not cut your guaranteed benefits. Let me repeat that: They will not cut your guaranteed benefits, period. I'd be wary of anybody who claimed otherwise.

Projected Savings on Insurance Premiums Under the Reform Law

In 2014, annual premiums are projected to fall compared to what they would have been without the Affordable Care Act. These savings could be as much as $2,300 for middle-income families purchasing through Exchanges. A low-income family of four with an income of $33,525 could save as much as $9,900 in premiums and $5,000 in cost sharing due to the extra help from new tax credits and cost sharing assistance. Small businesses, on average, could save up to $350 per family policy due to lower costs in the Exchanges and could get tax credits for up to 50 percent of their premiums. Even large businesses will likely see lower premiums of $200 per family due to an increase in healthier enrollees. After 2014, analysts predict that premium growth should slow because of the Affordable Care Act, adding another $2,000 to family savings by 2019.

US Department of Health and Human Services, "Health Insurance Premiums: Past High Costs Will Become the Present and Future Without Health Reform," January 28, 2011. www.healthcare.gov.

So these are the reforms that take effect right away. These reforms won't give the Government more control over your health care. They certainly won't give the insurance companies more control over your health care. These reforms give you more control over your health care. And that's only the beginning.

An Insurance Exchange Will Increase Coverage

That's only the beginning. After more than a decade, we finally renewed the Indian Health Care Improvement Act. And the other changes I'm signing into law will take several years to implement fully, but that's because this is a difficult, complex issue and we want to get it right.

One of these reforms is the creation of a health insurance exchange. This is one of the most important reforms—and by the way, originally, I should point out, a Republican idea. Imagine that.

The idea is, is that right now there are a lot of people out there buying health insurance on their own or small businesses buying health insurance on their own. They don't work for a big company, they're not part of a big pool, so they have no leverage; they've got no bargaining power with insurance companies. But now what we're going to do is create exchanges all across the country where uninsured people, small businesses, they're going to be able to purchase affordable, quality insurance. They will be part of a big pool, just like Federal employees are part of a big pool. They'll have the same choice of private health insurance that Members of Congress get for themselves. That's going to happen as a consequence of this legislation.

And when this exchange is up and running, not only because of better bargaining power will they see their premiums reduced, will people get a better deal, but millions of people who still can't afford it are going to get tax breaks so they can afford coverage. And this represents the largest middle class tax cut for health care in our history. And it's going to mean that millions of people can get health care that don't have it currently.

There Is Still Work to Do

Now, for those of us who fought so hard for these reforms and believe in them so deeply, I have to remind you our job is not finished. We're going to have to see to it that these reforms are administered fairly and responsibly. And this includes rooting out waste and fraud and abuse in the system. That's how we'll extend the life of Medicare and bring down health care costs for families and businesses and governments. And in fact, it is through these reforms that we achieve the biggest reduction in our long-term deficits since the Balanced Budget Act of the 1990s.

So for all those folks out there who are talking about being fiscal hawks and didn't do much when they were in power, let's just remind them that according to the Congressional Budget Office, this represents over a trillion dollars of deficit reduction, but it's being done in a smart way.

And for those who've been suspicious of reform—and there are a lot of wonderful folks out there who, with all the noise, got concerned because of the misinformation that has marred this debate—I just repeat: Don't take my word for it. Go to our web site, whitehouse.gov; go to the web sites of major news outlets out there; find out how reform will affect you. And I'm confident that you will like what you see: a commonsense approach that maintains the private insurance system, but makes it work for everybody; makes it work not just for the insurance companies, but makes it work for you.

So that's what health reform is all about. Now, as long as a road that this has been, we all know our journey is far from over. There's still the work to do to rebuild this economy. There's still work to do to spur on hiring. There's work to do to improve our schools and make sure every child has a decent education. There's still work to do to reduce our dependence on foreign oil. There's more work to do to provide greater economic security to a middle class that has been struggling for a decade.

So this victory does not erase the many serious challenges we face as a nation. Those challenges have been allowed to linger for years, even decades, and we're not going to solve them all overnight.

But as we tackle all these other challenges that we face, as we continue on this journey, we can take our next steps with new confidence, with a new wind at our backs. Because we know it's still possible to do big things in America. Because we know it's still possible to rise above the skepticism, to rise above the cynicism, to rise above the fear. Because we know it's still possible to fulfill our duty to one another and to future generations.

So, yes, this has been a difficult 2 years. There will be difficult days ahead. But let us always remember the lesson of this day and the lesson of history: That we, as a people, do not shrink from a challenge; we overcome it. We don't shrink from our responsibilities; we embrace it. We don't fear the future; we shape the future. That's what we do. That's who we are. That makes us the United States of America.

"From page 1 to page 906, ObamaCare
is chock full of expensive, intrusive, and
downright scary programs."

Health Care Reform Law Expands Government Control

Michael Tennant

In the following viewpoint, Michael Tennant, software developer and writer, predicts the Patient Protection and Affordable Care Act (PPACA)—also commonly referred to by opponents as "ObamaCare"—will allow the US government to expand its reach into the lives of its citizens. Tennant claims the law compels all Americans to acquire health care, and those who cannot afford to pay for it will be granted taxpayer-subsidized care. He also insists the PPACA has certain provisions that could allow the government to regulate personal behaviors (such as smoking) and check up on individuals to see if they are obeying specific mandates—all in the name of ensuring community health. To monitor the public and devise strategies to implement these measures, the PPACA creates vast new government bureaucracies that will effectively micromanage people's health, Tennant claims. For these reasons, he calls for the repeal of this intrusive and expensive act.

As you read, consider the following questions:

1. Why does Tennant believe the Working Group on Health

Michael Tennant, "The New World of ObamaCare," *New American*, vol. 26, no. 16, August 16, 2010. Used by permission.

Care Quality is a bureaucracy devoted to more than just health care?

2. What reservations does Tennant have about the Maternal, Infant, and Early Childhood Home Visiting Programs?

3. Besides granting the government another means of keeping tabs on citizens, who does Tennant claim will benefit from the PPACA's section 4204 that provides home vaccination visits?

By now most Americans are familiar with the broad outline of ObamaCare: Everyone is required by law to purchase health insurance, with a tax penalty assessed upon those who fail to comply. Insurers may not refuse to cover those with pre-existing conditions nor charge them higher rates. The federal government is expanding its role in providing health insurance. And did I mention that all of this is supposedly going to reduce both healthcare costs and the federal deficit?

Of course, with a law that is over 900 pages long and contains hundreds of mandates, it may be months or even years before all the ramifications of the law are understood. Some of the mandates are already widely known, such as the requirement that chain restaurants post nutrition information about their menu items or the 10-percent tax on tanning salon services. However, it may very well be that the less widely known portions of the law are also the most dangerous, which may explain why they were kept out of public view in contravention of candidate Barack Obama's repeated assurances that the entire healthcare debate would be conducted in public and broadcast on C-Span.

A Potential Tool of Oppression

Among the obscure but dangerous provisions in the Patient Protection and Affordable Care Act (the official—and disingenuous—name for ObamaCare) are numerous provisions that, said Art Thompson, CEO of The John Birch Society, "will intrude on every aspect of life in America, from cradle to grave." They include everything from a national healthcare strategy to home visitations by government agents, possibly including forced immunizations, to "Community Transformation Grants"—all designed to alter Americans' lifestyles to conform to the whims of bureaucrats in Washington.

The law itself is (probably intentionally) vague about how all these mandates are to be carried out; the details are left mostly to federal agencies that are much less accountable to the voters than Congress. Therefore, many of the suggestions in the following paragraphs as to how these mandates will play out are based not on explicit language in the legislation itself, or (obviously) the yet-to-be-issued regulations, but on an informed understanding of how governments can turn seemingly beneficent laws into tools of oppression. If anything, much of what is suggested in this article is actually *less* radical than what President Obama and fellow Democrats have said they wish to accomplish, namely a single-payer health insurance scheme at the federal level.

Moving Toward Socialized Medicine

Obama himself, in a 2003 speech, said that he'd "like to see" the United States adopt a "single-payer health care plan, a universal health care plan."

His Secretary of State, Hillary Clinton, of course, attempted to foist a single-payer government healthcare system on Americans back in 1993 and '94. Many other Clinton administration figures are prominent members of the Obama administration.

Obama's recently appointed head of the Centers for Medicare and Medicaid Services, Donald Berwick, has openly praised the British National Health Service for not leaving healthcare to "play out in the darkness of private enterprise." Berwick added that "any healthcare that is just, equitable, civilized, and humane must, *must* redistribute wealth from the richer among us to the poorer and the less fortunate. Excellent healthcare is by definition redistributional." Berwick is also a proponent of government rationing of healthcare, saying, "The decision is not whether or not we will ration care. The decision is whether we will ration with our eyes open." Tellingly, Obama took the occasion of a Senate recess to appoint Berwick, bypassing Senate confirmation hearings that would surely have publicized Berwick's socialized-medicine *bona fides* and possibly have sunk his nomination.

Thus, it is almost impossible to be too alarmist about the intentions of ObamaCare and its proponents. When government controls the healthcare system from top to bottom, it is naturally going to attempt to manipulate every aspect of people's lives in order to keep costs down; and for those who become ill despite the state's best efforts to force them to be healthy, care can—and will—be denied. This is already happening in Berwick's beloved British healthcare system, where, for example, life-saving drugs are withheld from patients because the government deems them too costly—and then threatens patients who try to purchase the drugs out of their own pockets with the loss of all their health-care benefits.

A New Bureaucracy to Micromanage Health Care

Perhaps the most ominous of the obscure-but-dangerous provisions in ObamaCare is found in Sections 3011 through 3015. This portion of the law instructs the Secretary of Health and Human Services to "establish a national strategy to improve the delivery of health care services, patient health outcomes, and population health." Along with the strategy, the law requires "a comprehensive strategic plan to achieve the priorities" established by Congress. The strategic plan includes "agency-specific strategic plans to achieve national priorities," "annual benchmarks for each relevant agency," and "strategies to align public and private payers with regard to quality and patient safety efforts." In short, the federal government is going to micromanage the healthcare sector in an effort to achieve its desired outcomes, and it is going to force private insurers to participate in this micromanagement—part of the price they will pay for having Uncle Sam hand them a captive market.

In order to implement the national strategy, the law instructs the President to "convene a working group to be known as the Interagency Working Group on Health Care Quality." This new bureaucracy includes senior-level representatives from 23 named federal agencies "and any other Federal agencies and departments . . . as determined by the President." Among the agencies included in the working group are the Department of Commerce, the Coast Guard, the Federal Bureau of Prisons, the National Highway Traffic Safety Administration, the Federal Trade Commission, the Department of Labor, the Department of Defense, and the Department of Education—a strong indication that this is concerned with far more than simply ensuring that patients are treated well.

Likewise, Section 4001 of the act instructs the President to "establish, within the Department of Health and Human Services, a council to be known as the 'National Prevention, Health Promotion and Public Health Council.'" President Obama issued an executive order to carry out this provision on June 10 [2010].

The council is chaired by the Surgeon General and consists of senior-level representatives from 12 named federal agencies and "the head of any other Federal agency that the chairperson determines is appropriate."

The purposes of the council include: (1) to coordinate "prevention, wellness and health promotion practices;" (2) to "develop a national prevention, health promotion, public health, and integrative health care strategy;" (3) to "provide recommendations to the President and Congress concerning . . . changes in Federal policy to achieve national wellness, health promotion, and public health goals, including the reduction of tobacco use, sedentary behavior, and poor nutrition;" and (4) to propose policies "for the promotion of transformative models of prevention, integrative health, and public health on individual and community levels across the United States." There will be "a list of national priorities" and "specific science-based initiatives" to "address lifestyle behavior modification" with regard to "smoking cessation, proper nutrition, appropriate exercise, mental health, behavioral health, substance use disorder, and domestic violence screenings."

"It's a horror even to think that they would put that in there, that they are going to start regulating personal behavior," Rep. Ron Paul (R-Texas), himself a physician, told *The New American*. "But these people believe in it, and this is why it's so bad to allow government to get inside the door. . . . They get their foot in the door, and then they say, 'Oh, we're paying for it, so we're going to tell you how to live.'"

Regulating Behavior

In other words, ObamaCare has just turned the United States into one giant psychiatric laboratory, and Americans are the rats stuck inside and subjected to "behavior modification" until we stop smoking (wonder if this applies to the President, who still hasn't kicked the habit), take our vaccines and stop eating Twinkies, take up jogging, quit ingesting substances that the big pharmaceutical companies can't patent, and tell Uncle Sam when we stopped beating our wives. Is this really what all those folks clamoring for healthcare reform wanted? If so, it serves as further proof of [journalist and culture critic] H.L. Mencken's maxim that "democracy is the theory that the common people know what they want, and deserve to get it good and hard."

Section 4101 provides for grants for school-based health centers, which will offer "comprehensive health assessments, diagnosis, and treatment of minor, acute, and chronic medical conditions" and "mental health and substance use disorder assessments, crisis intervention, counseling, treatment, and referral to a continuum of services including emergency psychiatric care, community support programs, inpatient care, and outpatient programs."

Will parents' rights be respected in all this? Will their children be treated without their knowledge?

The "primary function" of existing school-based health centers "is to circumvent parental involvement in the important area of directing a child's healthcare," Gregory Hession, a Massachusetts attorney specializing in family and juvenile law, said in an e-mail. The programs "sexualize children with condom giveaways, homosexual advocacy programs, and age-inappropriate instruction to children, even very young ones, about sexual activity," said Hession. "These clinics even allow and promote statutory rape" and refer students to abortion clinics and provide transportation to the clinics, Hession added, pointing out that all of this is done "in complete secrecy."

And what of mental health assessments? Hession stated that much of the mental health screening that already takes place in schools appears to be "fostered by psychiatrists with financial ties to large drug companies that offer psychotropic drugs which are almost invariably prescribed for any small perceived personality problem," the result being "that many children are now required, as a contingency for attending school, to lake powerful psychotropic drugs for such invented maladies as attention deficit disorder."

With school-based health clinics already engaged in such unsavory practices, federal funding and mandates can only lead to even worse, and more widespread, abuses.

More Intrusive Measures

Nothing less than the "transformation" of communities is the modest goal of Section 4201, which creates a grant program for state and local governments and nonprofit organizations "to reduce chronic disease rates, prevent the development of secondary conditions, address health disparities, and develop a stronger evidence-base of effective prevention programming." Each grantee must develop a "community transformation plan," which may include such things as:

- creating healthier school environments, including increasing healthy food options, physical activity opportunities, promotion of healthy lifestyle, emotional wellness, and prevention curricula, and activities to prevent chronic diseases;

• creating the infrastructure to support active living and access to nutritious foods in a safe environment;

• developing and promoting programs targeting a variety of age levels to increase access to nutrition, physical activity and smoking cessation, improve social and emotional wellness, enhance safety in a community, or address any other chronic disease priority area identified by the grantee;

• assessing and implementing worksite wellness programming and incentives;

• working to highlight healthy options at restaurants and other food venues;

• prioritizing strategies to reduce racial and ethnic disparities, including social, economic, and geographic determinants of health; and

• addressing special populations needs, including all age groups and individuals with disabilities, and individuals in both urban and rural areas.

Imagine telling the Founding Fathers that the federal government would someday be concerning itself with restaurant menus and workplace stress! They would have laughed you right out of Philadelphia. Yet here we are, with the feds doing just that and much, much more.

Just what is "emotional wellness," and how is the government going to see to it that people attain it? Surely it isn't by cutting bureaucracy and spending, bringing the troops home, and reducing taxes, though those are the surest ways to make (almost) everyone happier. . . .

Then there's that business about "reducing disparities." The intention, undoubtedly, is to see to it that those who do not have health insurance receive it—and that those who have too much of it, as Washington sees it, are forced to make do with less; hence the tax penalties applied to so-called Cadillac plans. Subsidizing insurance for some will only encourage them to make more use of the healthcare system, putting upward pressure on prices and hastening the day that Berwick and others of his ilk begin rationing care for them. Punishing those with the best insurance plans will ensure that some of those individuals are unable to afford the care they need, which is just rationing by other means. The result: We all end up in the mushy middle, with just as much care as the government deems necessary to keep us from being too much of a strain on the system. For those who do become too ill and therefore too expensive for the government to keep, denial of treatment is an easy fix.

Individuals who use community health centers funded by the government may also be given a government-sanctioned "individualized wellness plan" under Section 4206, which establishes a demonstration project for this purpose. Undoubtedly this will be declared a success, and soon all Americans can expect a Washington-mandated plan for their lives, to control such things as alcohol and tobacco use, weight, blood pressure, nutritional supplement usage (but only those supplements "that have health claims approved by the Secretary"), stress, and exercise.

Invading Homes and Schools

One need not go to a health clinic to be subjected to federal healthcare intrusions, either. At least two portions of the act actually provide for government agents to come into individuals' homes to see to it that they are obeying Washington's directives.

The first of these is Section 2951, entitled "Maternal, Infant, and Early Childhood Home Visiting Programs." This section requires all states to perform a needs assessment that identifies at-risk communities and "the quality and capacity of existing programs or initiatives for early childhood home visitation." States can then apply for grants to establish early childhood home visitation programs.

The programs will target high-risk communities first, with "high-risk" defined as "eligible families who reside in communities in need of such services," followed by eligible families with low incomes, pregnant women under 21 years old, "a history of child abuse or neglect . . . or interactions with child welfare services" (not evidence of actual abuse, mind you; just a visit from government agents on an anonymous tip will suffice), "a history of substance abuse," "users of tobacco products" (light up and expect a visit from your friendly neighborhood G-man), "children with low student achievement," "children with developmental delays or disabilities," or "individuals who are serving or formerly served in the Armed Forces." That just about covers everyone.

"This section of the law is designed to circumvent the Fourth Amendment to the U.S. Constitution, and give government agents a plausible excuse to enter homes without a warrant, with the ultimate goal of reporting the family to child protective services," said Hession. The child-protection agents then have every incentive to take children from their families, as evidenced by the fact that over half a million children are now in child protection agency custody in the United States.

The law lays out specific desired outcomes for individual families, many of which sound good. Who could oppose improvements in mothers' and babies' health, children's development, parenting skills, school readiness and academic achievement, crime and domestic violence rates, and family economic self-sufficiency? The detailed regulations established by federal and state bureaucrats to accomplish these general outcomes, however, may not be so benign.

For example, what specific "improvements in parenting skills" might government agents wish to impose on those they visit? Will spanking children or even speaking sharply to them be permitted? What if parents try to inculcate specific moral or religious precepts in their children? Hession noted that home-schoolers and parents who believe in corporal punishment

Obamacare: The First Six Months

Massive bureaucracy. Disinformation campaigns. Blatant power plays. The politicization of decisions that should be made with a focus on patient care. The use of government power to threaten citizens and their livelihood.

This is what Obamacare has brought us. And that's just in its first six months.

James C. Capretta, "The Anatomy of a Hostile Government Takeover," National Review, *September 28, 2010. www.nationalreview.com.*

are already among the most targeted by state child protection agencies.

It is already known that government programs to improve school readiness are of little benefit. Gains made in Head Start, the most famous of these programs, do not last much beyond first grade. Why, then, would anyone expect the government to be able to offer parents expert advice on how to prepare their children for school?

Worse yet, how will "school readiness" and "child academic achievement" be measured? What will happen to families whose children fail to meet the government's arbitrary standards? As the Birch Society's Art Thompson perceptively pointed out,

The idea of school readiness and academic achievement provides the excuse for government agents to nullify parental prerogatives for private and home schooling. Since they can test the preschool children, mold the tests of how and what the children should be taught, they can use this information to try and force you to send your children to government institutions.

In fact, school readiness is one of the key reasons boosters of universal pre-kindergarten cite for their support of extending government schooling to an earlier age. Among those who favor universal pre-kindergarten are Hillary Clinton—she of "It Takes a Village to Raise a Child" and the anti-parental-rights Children's Defense Fund—and President Obama. *Prima facie* evidence that it's a bad idea. . . .

Compulsory Immunizations

As if that weren't bad enough, Section 4204 actually provides for home visits from government functionaries for the purpose of providing immunizations (a demonstration program for the time being but with the intent "to continue and expand such program").

The recent H1N1 hoopla demonstrates how the government, with the enthusiastic backing of vaccine manufacturers, can manufacture a health crisis and then use it to encourage or even force people to be vaccinated. The *Washington Post* reported on June 4 [2010] that two separate reports from Europe "accused the [World Health Organization] of exaggerating the threat posed by the virus and failing to disclose possible influence by the pharmaceutical industry on its recommendations for how countries should respond." That exaggeration of the so-called pandemic and the WHO's accompanying recommendations led many Americans to be vaccinated needlessly, including some who were coerced by the government, such as healthcare workers in New York.

Now imagine that same scenario playing out under a program in which the federal government gives grants to states to (1) provide "immunization reminders or recalls for target populations," (2) educate "targeted populations and health care providers concerning immunizations in combination with one or more other interventions," (3) subsidize immunizations, (4) promote immunizations, (5) provide for "home visits" that may include "provision of immunization," and (6) create an electronic database for all states to access immunization records—all provisions of the Patient Protection and Affordable Health Care Act. How easy it would be for governments to find out who hasn't volunteered to be vaccinated and to show up at the recalcitrant citizens' homes to give them their shots right then and there! How profitable it would be for vaccine manufacturers! . . .

People Control, Not Health Care

From page 1 to page 906, ObamaCare is chock full of expensive, intrusive, and downright scary programs such as these. The law gives the federal and state governments virtually unlimited power to interfere in Americans' lives, even within the confines of our own homes. (Hession noted that the act "is marbled with requirements that can be accomplished only by entry into private family homes.") It destroys individual self-reliance and, through a variety of provisions such as school-based health clinics and home visitation programs, the family unit. These are the foundations of the American Republic; without them the United States will become a society of helpless, dependent sheep with neither the desire nor the will to resist the state's relentless encroachments on our liberties.

These problems cannot be fixed merely by modifying a clause here and a proviso there. ObamaCare needs to be repealed in full before it can metastasize into a full-blown single-payer system. State-by-state nullification should also be undertaken. Then we can work on dismantling the rest of the federal healthcare behemoth. These are the only cures for what ails the American healthcare system.

> "I think we have already fairly well
> established the fact that when you strip
> out all the budget gimmicks and all the
> double accounting, ObamaCare is a
> budget buster."

Health Care Reform Law Will Increase the Federal Debt

Paul Ryan

Paul Ryan, a Republican and US representative from Wisconsin, is one of the architects of a 2012 budget proposal that most congressional Republicans are advocating as a response to President Barack Obama's budget plan. Part of the Republican budget plan—often called the Ryan budget—calls for changes to the Patient Protection and Affordable Care Act (PPACA), including repeal of tax credits, eliminating compulsory insurance, and the dismantling of the proposed health care exchanges. In the following viewpoint, a speech given to the House of Representatives on January 18, 2011, Ryan insists Congress should repeal the PPACA because its entitlements are too costly. According to Ryan, the administration has manipulated the expenditures for the PPACA to hide their true costs. Ryan maintains the PPACA will run at a deficit of $701 billion, which will have to be paid for by robbing other welfare programs or simply increasing the federal deficit.

Paul Ryan, "Should Congress Repeal the Patient Protection and Affordable Care Act? Pro," *Congressional Digest*, vol. 90, no. 3, March, 2011. Used by permission.

As you read, consider the following questions:
1. Who does Ryan believe should be in charge of health care decisions?
2. How much money does Ryan claim will be needed to finance the PPACA over the first ten years of its programs?
3. If the government chooses not to have the public finance the PPACA, what two welfare programs does Ryan believe will be "raided" to cover the PPACA expenses?

L et me just simply say why we are here. We are here because we heard the American people in the last election. We are here because we believe it's really important to do in office what you said you would do. We said we would have a straight up-or-down vote to repeal this health care law, and that's precisely what we are doing here today.

Now, why do we believe this? Because this health care law, if left in place, will accelerate our country's path toward bankruptcy. This health care law, if left in place, will do as the President's own chief actuary says it will do: It will increase health care costs.

The PPACA Is an Expensive Government Takeover

We are already seeing premiums go up across the board. We are already hearing from thousands of employers across the country who are talking about dropping their employer-sponsored health insurance, and we are already hearing about the lack of choices that consumers will get as this new law is put into place. This new law is a fiscal house of cards, and it is a health care house of cards. It does not make our health care system better. I would argue it makes it weaker.

There are two ways to attack this problem, and I want to say in the outset to my friends on the other side of the aisle, we agree that health care needs fixing. We agree that there are so many serious, legitimate problems in the health care system that need fixing. Affordable insurance, the uninsured, people with high health care costs and high health care risks—those need to be addressed. But we can fix what's not working in health care without breaking what's working in health care.

With that, I would simply say this: We believe we can get to the moment of having affordable health care for every American, regardless of preexisting conditions, without having the government take it over, without $1 trillion of a combination of Medicare benefit cuts and tax increases. We believe in this: Let's have health care reform put the patient in charge, not the government in charge.

We believe that health care ought to be individually based, and it ought to be patient centered.

There are two ways to go: Put the government in charge and have the government put in place rationing mechanisms to tighten the screws and ration health care; or put the consumer in charge and have providers compete for our business as patients, hospitals, doctors, and insurers. That's the system we want.

The Statistics Bespeak a Rise in the Federal Deficit

They're saying this is a jobs bill. Half a trillion dollars in tax increases creates jobs? The mandates, the taxes—that creates jobs?

Others have been saying, well, this isn't going to pass the Senate and the President's not going to sign it, so why bother doing that. If that's the logic we take on every bill we bring to the floor, then we ought to just go home. We think it's important to define ourselves with our actions, and that's why we're acting. We think this law should be totally repealed, and that's why we're doing this.

Let me speak to the fiscal house of cards as represented by this law. The minority is saying this reduces the deficit. Just look at the letter from CBO [Congressional Budget Office] to Speaker [of the House John] Boehner [OH-R]. It reduces the deficit by $143 billion over eight years; $230 billion over 10.

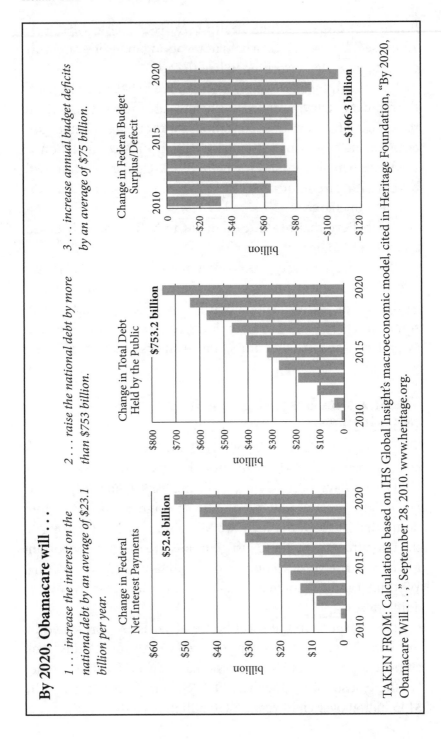

By 2020, Obamacare will . . .

1 . . . increase the interest on the national debt by an average of $23.1 billion per year.

Change in Federal
Net Interest Payments

$52.8 billion

2 . . . raise the national debt by more than $753 billion.

Change in Total Debt
Held by the Public

$753.2 billion

3 . . . increase annual budget deficits by an average of $75 billion.

Change in Federal Budget
Surplus/Deficit

−$106.3 billion

TAKEN FROM: Calculations based on IHS Global Insight's macroeconomic model, cited in Heritage Foundation, "By 2020, Obamacare Will . . .," September 28, 2010. www.heritage.org.

It does that if you manipulate the CBO. I've heard charges of Enron [Corporation] accounting [i.e., fraudulent accounting that hides true expenditures]. The only Enron accounting that's been employed here is the previous majority gave the CBO a bill full of smoke and mirrors and made them score that.

Well, here's what the CBO says. If you take away the smoke and mirrors, if you take away the fact that there's $70 billion in CLASS [Community Living Assistance Services and Supports] Act premiums that are being double-counted, $53 billion in Social Security taxes that are being double-counted, $115 billion in new appropriations required to hire the bureaucracy that wasn't counted, $398 billion in Medicare cuts that are being double-counted, and oh, let's not forget the fact that we're going to do the doctor fix, $208 billion, that we just discounted and ignored.

When you take away the smoke and the mirrors, this thing has a $701 billion deficit. If you don't believe me when I say it that way, how about this way: The CBO says this raises the debt.

Now, how is that different where they say on one hand the bill lowers the deficit but on the other hand it raises the debt? Because when the CBO looks at whether or not a measure raises the debt, they can look at everything. They look at the interplay of all fiscal policies to determine its effects on the debt. When they score a particular bill and its effects on the deficit, they look at what you put in front of them, all the smoke, all the mirrors, the double-counting, the non-counting, the discounting, and they give you that answer.

Forcing Business to Drop Insurance

So if this bill actually lowers the deficit, how on Earth can it then increase the debt? You know why? Because you have to play a phony trick with all this double-counting to do that. What does this bill ultimately do when you really look at it all? This bill blows a hole through the deficit. When you look at the first 10 years, this bill is a $1.4 trillion increase. That's because you have 10 years of tax increases and Medicare cuts to pay for six years of spending. But when you actually look at the full 10 years of implementation of this law, $2.6 trillion in spending—$2.6 trillion.

Let me just say this as far as jobs and the effects of this health care bill. I had a very alarming conversation with a very large employer in Wisconsin not too long ago, a privately held company with thousands of employees. She takes good care of her employees.

She said to me, I believe it's my obligation to offer health insurance to my employees, but my two competitors, my publicly traded competitors, have already said they're dumping their employees. Instead of paying $17,000 a year for employee health care, they're going to pay a $2,000 fine. That's a $15,000 difference that her competitor will have as a competitive advantage against you.

So what did she say? "I have no choice. I'm dumping my employees into this exchange." And thousands of employers are making the same decision. This should be repealed.

A Nonfundable Program

Second, either we are financing this entitlement or raiding the Social Security and Medicare funds—you can't do both. If you are going to fund the entitlement with these revenues, then you are consigning to raid Social Security and Medicare.

I think we have already fairly well established the fact that when you strip out all the budget gimmicks and all the double accounting, ObamaCare is a budget buster. But let's take a look at where we are as a country.

We have a debt crisis coming in America, and the primary reason why we have this mountain of debt is because of our already existing health care entitlements, which have a massive unfunded liability. So what did the previous majority do? They just put two new unfunded, open-ended entitlements on top.

Now, a lot of people on the other side of the aisle said health care is a right and we are giving it to the people. Well, if we declare such things as a right to be given to us by government, then it's government's right to ration these things; it's government's right to regulate these things; it's government's right to pick and choose winners and losers. Health care is too important for that. I want to be in control of my and my family's health care. I want individuals to be in control of their health care and their destiny.

We have to ask ourselves when we create these new programs how much of our children's future and our grandchildren's future are we willing to sacrifice to give them this mountain of debt that is getting worse by the passage and creation of this law. This, of all reasons, is why we should vote to repeal.

> "CBO [Congressional Budget Office]
> estimates the legislation will reduce
> the deficit by $143 billion over the ten
> years from 2010 through 2019."

Health Care Reform Law Will Reduce the Federal Debt

Paul N. Van de Water and James R. Horney

In the viewpoint that follows, Paul N. Van de Water and James R. Horney claim that the Patient Protection and Affordable Care Act passed in 2010 will reduce health care expenses and the federal deficit. The authors refute claims that health care spending under the new law has been miscounted in order to deceive Congress and the public; they insist the program accounts for its own expenditures and will shrink the federal deficit by $143 billion over the first ten years from health care savings alone. Van de Water and Horney also insist that the law will help keep Medicare solvent for a longer period of time. A former employee of the Congressional Budget Office, Paul N. Van de Water is a senior fellow at the Center on Budget and Policy Priorities, an organization that helps inform expert and public debate on federal budget and tax policies. James R. Horney is the vice president for federal fiscal policy at the Center on Budget and Policy Priorities.

Paul N. Van de Water and James R. Horney, "Health Reform Will Reduce the Deficit: Charges of Budgetary Gimmickry Are Unfounded," Center on Budget and Policy Priorities, March 25, 2010. Used by permission.

As you read, consider the following questions:

1. According to the authors, how will the new excise tax on high-cost insurance plans help fund Social Security and thus reduce deficit spending on that program?

2. In Van de Water and Horney's opinion, why do critics continue to point to the sustainable growth rate formula as evidence that Congress will not permit Medicare savings measures to be implemented?

3. How do the authors account for the fact that health care savings will accrue even if covering more uninsured people will result in higher expenditures?

Despite an official estimate by the Congressional Budget Office (CBO) to the contrary, some critics of the new health reform legislation—such as Rep. Paul Ryan [of Wisconsin] and former CBO director and [Senator John] McCain [of Arizona] campaign adviser Douglas Holtz-Eakin—charge that it will not reduce federal budget deficits because it relies on budgetary gimmicks or games. Careful analysis of these charges shows them to be misleading or inaccurate. They do not withstand scrutiny.

CBO estimates the legislation will reduce the deficit by $143 billion over the ten years from 2010 through 2019. In the following decade, 2020 through 2029, it estimates that the legislation will reduce the deficit by an estimated one-half of 1 percent of gross domestic product (GDP), or about $1.3 trillion. CBO also anticipates that health reform "would probably continue to reduce budget deficits relative to those under current law in subsequent decades, assuming that all of its provisions continue to be fully implemented."

We now examine the specific claims about budgetary gimmicks and games one by one.

Short-Term and Long-Term Savings

Claim: Health reform covers up long-term deficit increases by front-loading revenues and back-loading spending.

Fact: Health reform will reduce deficits in the legislation's second ten years and in subsequent decades.

In claiming that health reform front-loads revenues and back-loads spending, critics selectively cite just a few provisions and fail to consider the legislation as a whole. The assertion that short-term gimmickry covers up long-term deficit increases is flatly contradicted by CBO's assessment that the legislation will reduce the deficit in its second ten years and in subsequent decades.

Claim: The legislation uses revenues from Social Security and premiums from long-term care insurance to offset the cost of health reform.

Fact: Health reform reduces the deficit even without counting long-term care insurance premiums and additional Social Security payroll tax collections.

CBO and the Joint Committee on Taxation have concluded that the health reform legislation will reduce employer spending on health insurance, in part because the new excise tax on high-cost insurance plans will lead employers to shift some employee compensation from health insurance to cash wages. Workers will pay Social Security payroll contributions and income taxes on the additional wages.

The legislation also establishes a new, voluntary program of long-term care insurance, called the CLASS Act. Benefit payments from CLASS will be fully financed by premiums that beneficiaries pay and interest earnings. In its early years, as the program starts up, premium collections will substantially exceed benefit payments.

Congressional leaders crafted the health reform bill so that it would be *fully paid for without relying on these additional Social Security payroll contributions or the CLASS Act premiums.* The CBO estimate clearly shows that if one excludes the net revenues of $29 billion from Social Security contributions and $70 billion from CLASS Act premiums, health reform still reduces the deficit by $44 billion over the first ten years.

Medicare Savings

Claim: Medicare savings are double-counted.

Fact: The Medicare savings in the legislation both reduce the budget deficit and extend the life of Medicare's Hospital Insurance trust fund. Recognizing that fact does not constitute double counting.

The health reform legislation contains provisions that slow the growth of Medicare spending—for example, by scaling back overpayments to private insurance plans that participate in Medicare, as Congress' expert advisory body on Medicare has recommended for years—and provisions that increase Medicare tax revenues. The provisions affecting the Hospital Insurance part of Medicare necessarily have two types of effects:

- Viewed from an overall federal budget perspective, they help pay for expanding health coverage for the uninsured and contribute to overall deficit reduction. CBO has estimated that the provisions in the health reform legislation, including the provisions affecting Medicare costs and revenues, will reduce the federal deficit both in the 2010–2019 period and thereafter.

- Viewed from the perspective of Medicare's Hospital Insurance (HI) trust fund, these provisions reduce expenditures out of the fund, increase its income, increase the balances in the fund, and prolong the fund's life. The Office of the Actuary at the Centers for Medicare & Medicaid Services (CMS) has estimated that the Senate-passed bill (which has now been signed into law) will extend the solvency of the HI trust fund by ten years.

Both of these results flow automatically from the nature of the federal budget and the trust funds, and the normal, longstanding accounting rules that apply to them. No double-counting occurs.

Deficit-reduction legislation has been accounted for in exactly the same way in previous Congresses under both political parties.

For example, both the Balanced Budget Act of 1997 and the Deficit Reduction Act of 2005 (both of which were passed by Republican Congresses) included Medicare savings that reduced the federal deficit *and* improved the solvency of Medicare's HI trust fund. No claims of double-counting were raised when these bills were enacted.

Claim: Congress doesn't allow Medicare savings to go into effect.

Fact: The vast majority of the provisions enacted in the past 20 years to produce Medicare savings were successfully implemented.

A careful examination of the historical record demonstrates that Congress has repeatedly adopted measures to produce considerable savings in Medicare *and has let them take effect.* In an earlier analysis, we examined every piece of major Medicare legislation enacted in the last 20 years. Four pieces of legislation included significant Medicare savings. Virtually all of the Medicare savings in three of these pieces of legislation—the 1990, 1993, and 2005 budget reconciliation bills—were successfully implemented. In addition, nearly *four-fifths* of the savings enacted in the fourth piece of legislation—the Balanced Budget Act of 1997—were implemented despite the fact that a balanced budget was achieved in 1998 (four years earlier than the target date of the legislation) and Medicare spending slowed far more than had been projected when the legislation passed. In fact, for the first time in history, Medicare spending in 1999 was lower than it had been the year before.

In short, the claim that Congress does not allow Medicare savings to take effect is false. It is thoroughly refuted by the historical record.

The one significant exception to this pattern of Medicare savings taking effect is what happened to the badly designed "sustainable growth rate" (SGR) formula, which set payments to physicians and was enacted as part of the 1997 Balanced Budget Act. Contrary to common misconceptions, the SGR provision was originally expected to produce only a *small* amount of savings—

less than 5 percent of the total Medicare savings in the Balanced Budget Act, or only $12 billion over ten years. The SGR formula was subsequently blocked by Congress when it turned out that it would have had the unintended effect of cutting payments well below doctors' actual costs of providing services. And even though Congress has not allowed the *full* cuts required under the SGR formula to take effect, it has still cut the physician reimbursement rate substantially: the current reimbursement rate in 2010 is *17 percent below* the rate for 2001, adjusted for medical care inflation.

Those who ignore all of the other Medicare savings provisions enacted over the past 20 years, single out the SGR experience, and cite it as evidence that Congress does not allow intended Medicare savings to materialize have jumped to a faulty conclusion inconsistent with the record.

It also should be noted that most of the Medicare savings provisions in the health reform legislation are similar to the types of Medicare provisions that Congress has enacted in the past that have indeed taken effect, and differ markedly from the blunt-instrument design of the SGR cut. Furthermore, as Goldman-Sachs [investment bank] has noted in a recent analysis of the health reform bill, there is little likelihood that the circumstances that prevailed in the late 1990s will recur. At that time, the achievement of a balanced budget and the projection of continued budget surpluses helped convince the President and Congress to undo a small portion of the Medicare savings enacted in 1997.

Claim: The estimate for health reform should include the cost of fixing the sustainable growth rate (SGR) payment formula for physicians.

Fact: The cost of fixing the SGR formula is entirely unrelated to health reform; all of its cost would remain if health reform were repealed tomorrow.

Some critics complain that the CBO cost estimate for health reform is misleading because the legislation does not include a permanent fix to the broken SGR payment formula for physicians. Since Congress will likely continue to prevent the SGR from taking effect, they say, Congress should consider the cost of such action as part of the cost of health reform.

Indeed, Congress likely will never let the full SGR cuts take effect, and it probably won't offset the cost of scrapping them. But that cost is neither part of, nor in any way a result of, health reform. *The federal government will incur this cost regardless of health reform, not because of it.* This fact is undeniable: if health reform legislation had not been enacted, the full SGR cost would remain. To be sure, it would be better if Congress offset the cost of cancelling the SGR cuts. But that issue is separate from the question of how much health reform itself reduces the deficit.

All Spending Is Accounted For

Claim: Health reform doesn't "bend the cost curve" because it extends health coverage to 32 million uninsured, which increases health care costs.

Fact: Health reform includes an extensive array of provisions to slow the growth of health care costs.

This claim confuses the short-run and long-run effects of health reform. Because people who lack health insurance use fewer health care services, expanding insurance coverage will, by itself, increase health care spending in the short term. It is therefore no surprise that the chief actuary of the Centers for Medicare & Medicaid Services [CMS] has estimated that the health reform legislation—which will extend coverage to two-thirds of the uninsured—will increase national health expenditures by 1.7 percent in 2016, when its coverage expansions will be fully phased in.

Although covering the uninsured will necessarily increase the *level* of national health expenditures at first, the key question is what will happen to the *rate of growth* of health expenditures thereafter. Even a modest slowdown in annual cost growth will more than offset the initial cost increase within a short period of time. The CMS actuary also finds that health reform will indeed slow the rate of growth of national health expenditures after an initial increase. Furthermore, CBO estimates that by the decade after 2019, the total federal budgetary commitment to health care—the sum of net federal outlays for health programs and tax preferences for health care—will be *lower* than it would have been if the health reform legislation were not enacted.

The health reform legislation includes an extensive array of provisions that hold considerable potential for slowing the growth in health care costs even more over the long haul. The legislation begins to move in most areas that health policy experts consider promising avenues for reducing the growth of health care spending and where specific steps can be identified. Health care experts agree that slowing the growth of health care costs will require an ongoing process of testing, experimentation, and rapid implementation of what is found to work. Enactment of the health reform legislation, which includes an array of demonstration projects to identify further ways to contain costs, begins that process.

Claim: The CBO cost estimate is misleading because it does not include discretionary spending that may be provided in future annual appropriation bills.

Fact: Future discretionary appropriations related to health reform are uncertain and may be accommodated without adding to total discretionary spending.

CBO treats mandatory spending and discretionary spending separately in estimating the cost of legislation. It does so for good reason. Mandatory spending, such as Medicare and Medicaid, continues from year to year unless new legislation is passed to reduce it. In contrast, discretionary spending, which covers most of the day-to-day operations of federal agencies, is provided for a year at a time in annual appropriations bills and is provided only to the extent that those bills make funding available. The CBO cost estimate for health reform appropriately includes all mandatory spending costs in its calculation of the effects of the legislation on the deficit, and provides a separate tabulation of the possible discretionary spending that could—contingent on future appropriations legislation—result from enactment of health reform.

CBO does not include discretionary spending in its assessment of the effects of legislation on the deficit because it cannot estimate either how much future discretionary funding Congresses will actually appropriate for any program or purpose or how any such appropriations would affect total discretionary spending. Congress operates in most years under a limit, set in the congressional budget resolution, on the total amount of discretionary funding that can be appropriated for that year. As a result, any increases in discretionary funding related to health reform may be accompanied by decisions to provide less funding for some other discretionary accounts, since Congress will need to remain within the operative ceiling on discretionary appropriations.

Discretionary spending for health reform falls into two categories. First is the cost to the Department of Health and Human Services, the Internal Revenue Service, and other federal agencies of *administering* the new arrangements to expand health insurance coverage and provide assistance to low- and moderate-income families. CBO estimates that these costs will be modest, totaling between $10 billion and $20 billion over the legislation's first ten years. This amount represents only a very small portion of the cost of the coverage expansions and could be easily accommodated by making offsetting reductions in other discretionary spending programs.

The second category of discretionary costs comprises authorizations for a variety of grant and other programs. CBO has reported that the health reform legislation includes $50 billion or more over ten years in authorizations with specified maximum funding levels, along with some other authorizations for which no level of funding is specified. But the effect of these authorizations on total spending is highly uncertain. Congress traditionally *authorizes* spending for many discretionary programs at much higher levels than are *actually appropriated*; indeed, many authorizations are never funded at all, because the Appropriations Committees cannot find room to fund them within the overall amount they are allowed to appropriate for the year. And unlike the administrative funding noted in the previous paragraph, these authorizations do not have to be funded; health reform is not at all contingent upon them. Finally, as with the administrative costs of health reform, any amounts that are eventually appropriated for these authorizations will need to fit within the overall discretionary spending ceilings Congress sets.

| "Seniors deserve better than what Obamacare gives them."

Health Care Reform Law Will Harm Seniors

Robert Moffitt

In the following viewpoint, Robert Moffitt claims that new policies under the Patient Protection and Affordable Care Act (PPACA) will negatively impact seniors. According to Moffitt, the new law will penalize seniors who are enrolled in Medicare Advantage—a plan that allows seniors who can afford it to pay for private health plans through a combination of Medicare funding and patient contributions—by cutting federal supports. This will force more seniors into standard Medicare plans that lack specific coverage (such as catastrophic care) seniors may need or simply desire. Moffitt also maintains that the PPACA cuts reimbursement rates to doctors, a practice that he fears will mean that some health care providers will terminate their Medicare-covered services, leaving patients without needed care. Moffitt is the director of the Center for Health Policy Studies at the Heritage Foundation, a conservative public policy think tank.

As you read, consider the following questions:

1. What will happen to Medicare Advantage enrollment by 2017, according to Moffitt?

Robert Moffitt, "Obamacare Will Be Devastating to Seniors," *Human Events*, March 31, 2010. Used by permission.

2. As Moffitt reports, what does the American Association of Medical Colleges predict the shortage of medical doctors will be by 2025?
3. As Moffitt explains, what will be the rate of the new Medicare tax imposed on unearned or investment income (that will take effect in 2013)?

According to surveys, no group of Americans is more skeptical of Obamacare than senior citizens—and with good reason.

While bits and pieces of the massive law are designed to appeal to seniors—more taxpayer subsidies for the Medicare drug benefit, for example—much of the financing over the initial ten years is siphoned off from an estimated $575 billion in projected savings to the Medicare program. Unless Medicare savings are captured and plowed right back into the Medicare program, however, the solvency of the Medicare program will continue to weaken. The law does not provide for that. Medicare is already burdened by an unfunded liability of $38 trillion.

Medicare Advantage plans, which currently attract almost one in four seniors, will see enrollment cut roughly in half over the next 10 years. Senior citizens will thus be more dependent on traditional Medicare than they are today and will have fewer healthcare choices.

Tax and Spend

Under the Medicare Modernization Act of 2003, Congress deliberately created a gap in Medicare drug coverage (the so-called "donut hole") in which seniors would be required to pay 100% of drug costs up to a specified amount. Obamacare provides a $250 rebate for seniors who fall into the "donut hole" and requires drug companies to provide a 50% discount on brand name prescriptions filled in the hole.

In 2011, Obamacare will also impose a new tax (a "fee") on the sale of these brand-name drugs in Medicare and other government health programs, ranging from $2.5 billion in 2011 to $4.1 billion in 2018. Meanwhile, the law will freeze payments to Medicare Advantage plans and restrict physicians from referring seniors in Medicare to specialty hospitals where physicians have an ownership interest. In 2013, the law eliminates the tax deductibility of the generous federal subsidy for employers who provide drug coverage for retirees. This could further undercut provision of employment-based prescription drug coverage for seniors.

Penalizing Medicare Advantage

With the freezing of Medicare Advantage payments in 2011, Congress has set the stage for a progressive reduction in seniors' access to, and choice of, the popular Medicare Advantage health plans.

In 2012, the law will begin reducing the federal benchmark payment for these plans. In 2014, these health plans must maintain a medical loss ratio of 85%, and the secretary of Health and Human Services is to suspend and even terminate enrollment in plans that miss this target.

Enrollment in Medicare Advantage by 2017 is estimated to be cut roughly in half, from a projected 14.8 million (under current law) to 7.4 million. Since there are serious gaps in Medicare coverage, including the absence of catastrophic protection, roughly nine out of ten seniors on traditional Medicare already need to purchase supplemental insurance, such as Medigap. Without Medicare Advantage, millions more seniors will have to go through the cumbersome process of paying two separate premiums for two health plans.

Growing Physician Shortage

In 2011, the new law provides a 10% Medicare bonus payment for primary care physicians and general surgeons in "shortage" areas. This is a tepid response to a growing problem.

With the retirement of 77 million baby boomers beginning in 2011, the Medicare program will have to absorb an unprecedented demand for medical services. For the next generation of senior citizens, finding a doctor will be more difficult and waiting times for doctor appointments are likely to be longer. The American Association of Medical Colleges projects a shortage of 124,000 doctors by 2025.

Obamacare has not ameliorated the growing problem of projected physician shortages and has surely made it worse. Under the new law, physicians will be even more dependent on flawed government payment systems for their reimbursement. Moreover, the congressionally designed Medicare physician-payment update formula, the Sustainable Growth Rate (SGR), initiates cuts that are so draconian that Congress goes through annual parliamentary gyrations to make sure its own handiwork does not go into effect.

Payment Cuts Mean Rationing

The new law also dramatically expands Medicaid, a poorly performing welfare program with low physician reimbursement rates, and this expansion will account for roughly half of the 34 million newly insured Americans. Furthermore, the law creates an Independent Payment Advisory Board, which will recommend measures to reduce Medicare spending.

Formally, the board is forbidden to make recommendations that ration care, increase revenues, or change Medicare beneficiaries' benefits, cost-sharing, eligibility or subsidies. For the board, reimbursement for doctors and other medical professionals seems the only target left. But payment cuts can effectively ration care.

Fewer Enticements for Providers

According to the Centers for Medicare and Medicaid Services (CMS):

> Over time, a sustained reduction in payment updates based on productivity expectations that are difficult to attain, would

cause Medicare payment rates to grow more slowly than—
and in a way unrelated to—the providers' cost of furnishing
services to beneficiaries. Thus, providers for whom Medicare
constitutes a substantial portion of their business could find it
difficult to remain profitable and, absent legislative intervention, might end their participation in the program (possibly
jeopardizing access to care for beneficiaries).

Indeed, creating a real problem for seniors, the CMS Actuary
estimates that roughly 15% of Medicare Part A providers—the
part of the Medicare program that pays hospital costs—would
become unprofitable within ten years.

Raising Taxes on Seniors

Under the new law, seniors are going to pay higher taxes. The
higher taxes on drugs (effective in 2011) and medical devices (effective in 2013) will affect seniors especially, as they are more
heavily dependent on those very products. Older people, of
course, have higher health costs than younger people. But the
existing tax deduction for medical expenses will be raised from
7.5% to 10% of adjusted gross income in 2013. The reduced tax
deductibility of medical expenses is waived for seniors only from
2013 to 2016. Likewise, older people have larger investments
than younger people—and thus high-income older persons will
be more heavily impacted by the new 3.8% Medicare tax imposed
on unearned or investment income (effective 2013).

New federal health insurance taxes—both the premium taxes
and the excise taxes—will also impact older workers and retirees. The federal premium tax (effective 2014) will be applicable
to Medicare Advantage plans and health plans offered to federal retirees in the Federal Employees Health Benefit Program
(FEHBP). Likewise, starting in 2018, there is a new 40% federal
excise tax on "Cadillac" health plans (defined as $10,220 for in-
dividual coverage and $27,500 for family coverage). This will also
apply to FEHBP plans, which enroll federal retirees.

No Real Reform at All

Forcing doctors and hospitals to comply with new rules and shaving reimbursement for treating senior citizens is not real reform. If Congress is going to reduce Medicare and impose a hard cap on Medicare payments to restrain per capita cost growth, at the very least it ought to channel those savings right back into the program to enhance Medicare's solvency and lay the fiscal foundation for real reform. Seniors deserve better than what Obamacare gives them.

> "New Mexico's seniors deserve the best
> medical system, with consistently
> excellent and affordable care. . . . The
> Patient Protection and Affordable Care
> Act will ensure they have access to such
> a system."

Health Care Reform Law Will Benefit Seniors

Jeff Bingaman

Jeff Bingaman is a US senator from New Mexico. In the viewpoint that follows, Bingaman explains why he supported the Patient Protection and Affordable Care Act (PPACA) and what he expects will be the benefits for seniors in his state and throughout the country. Bingaman claims the PPACA is aimed at cutting costs and improving quality in Medicare. He asserts that seniors will receive some free preventative care to help counter serious illness, and they will be given assistance with drug costs. Most importantly, he states that the new law will rein in Medicare Advantage plans to make sure these plans are not unfairly subsidized when compared to traditional Medicare plans. Bingaman insists that once the government begins imposing more efficiency on the delivery of health care, the costs to seniors will decrease.

Jeff Bingaman, "New Mexico Seniors Will Benefit from Health Reform," Jeff Bingaman Senate Web Page, May 3, 2010. http://bingaman.senate.gov.

As you read, consider the following questions:

1. According to Bingaman, when will the PPACA completely close the "donut hole" in Medicare drug coverage?
2. As Bingaman states, how much more do government subsidy payments to Medicare Advantage cost in comparison to traditional Medicare (on a nationwide average)?
3. How does the new law regulate nursing home care, according to the senator?

The Patient Protection and Affordable Care Act, enacted in March [2010], is comprehensive health insurance reform that will transform health care and health insurance. I supported this legislation because I believe it will make significant improvements to New Mexico's health care system.

These improvements will make a real difference to all New Mexicans, including our state's seniors. They build on my work over the years to strengthen Medicare, the backbone of care for 290,000 of our state's seniors and other beneficiaries. I worked to ensure that the new law preserves access to quality doctors by increasing Medicare reimbursement rates for physicians, particularly for primary care doctors, internal medicine physicians, and geriatricians.

Cutting Costs and Improving Quality

Although some critics have charged that Medicare benefits will be cut under the new law, this is not true. In fact, organizations that advocate for seniors, including AARP [a seniors' rights group formerly known as the American Association of Retired Persons] and the Medicare Rights Center, backed our reform effort.

There are six main ways that health care reform will significantly benefit New Mexico's seniors and other Medicare beneficiaries.

First, the law will protect and strengthen Medicare. It will improve quality and efficiency in the program while ending

An Advisory Board to Cut Wasteful Spending

The [2010 health care reform] law establishes an Independent Payment Advisory Board (IPAB) comprised of 15 full-time members to submit legislative proposals containing recommendations to reduce the per capita rate of growth in Medicare spending if spending exceeds a target growth rate, as determined by the CMS [Centers for Medicare and Medicaid Services] Chief Actuary. Recommendations from the Board to reduce spending could begin as early as 2014, although hospitals and hospices are exempt from further reductions through 2019. The Board's role is carefully circumscribed—its jurisdiction is over payment; it is prohibited from "rationing" care, increasing revenues, and changing benefits, eligibility or beneficiary cost-sharing.

Robert Berenson and John Holahan, "How Will the Patient Protection and Affordable Care Act Affect Seniors?" Urban Institute, July 2010. www.urban.org.

wasteful overpayments to insurance companies. As costs decrease and efficiency improves, seniors will not only receive higher quality care leading to better health outcomes but their own out-of-pocket share of Medicare costs will decrease.

Second, reform will reduce prescription drug costs for seniors. The Medicare drug benefit includes a broad interruption in coverage—often referred to as the "doughnut hole"—during which beneficiaries are responsible for 100 percent of the cost of drugs. I have long fought to eliminate the doughnut hole. I am very pleased that the new health reform law closes this gap completely by 2020.

In the meantime, seniors who hit the doughnut hole this year can immediately receive a $250 rebate checks to help with drug costs. And, next year, low- and middle-income beneficiaries will receive 50 percent discounts on many brand name drugs as well as partial coverage for generic drugs when in the doughnut hole.

Third, New Mexico's seniors will benefit from the new health reform law through free preventive care. Seniors will receive a free annual wellness visit and will not have to pay for any recommended preventive services, such as screenings for cancer, diabetes, and heart disease.

Bringing Medicare Advantage in Line with Traditional Medicare

Fourth, the new law reduces very serious overpayment to private insurance companies, which threatens the solvency of the Medicare trust fund and results in the increased costs to the majority of Medicare beneficiaries. Nationwide, Medicare Advantage [a plan that allowed seniors to purchase private health care through a combination of federal funding and patient contributions] costs taxpayers $1.14 for every dollar spent in traditional Medicare. In New Mexico, the ratio has been $1.28 to $1. To make up the difference, every man and woman across the country enrolled in traditional Medicare pays an average of $90 each year to subsidize their neighbors in Medicare Advantage. That means the 223,000 New Mexicans enrolled in traditional Medicare are subsidizing the health care costs for the 67,000 New Mexicans enrolled in Medicare Advantage. According to the nonpartisan Congressional Budget Office, these subsidies are a major factor threatening the solvency of Medicare.

It's important to note that the new law does not end Medicare Advantage, despite reports to the contrary. Instead, it moderately reduces Medicare Advantage payments so that they are more in line with traditional Medicare. The idea that Medicare

Advantage be paid in line with traditional Medicare is something that MedPAC—the nonpartisan commission that makes recommendations on Medicare to Congress—has long urged.

Under the new law, in New Mexico, private insurers offering Medicare Advantage will receive $1.13 for every $1 in traditional Medicare. If they meet new quality benchmarks they could receive as much as $1.18. Ultimately, this and other changes to the way we pay for Medicare will extend the solvency of Medicare Trust Fund from 2017 to 2026, protecting the program's benefits for both current and future recipients.

Benefits for Long-Term Care and Early Retirees

Fifth, the law makes significant headway in addressing the difficult long-term care gap facing many seniors and other Americans. The new law will help New Mexico expand support for Medicaid beneficiaries who need home and community-based care. It also creates a new voluntary long-term care insurance program available to working Americans. And, those needing care in nursing homes can rest easier knowing the law establishes new reporting and oversight requirements for nursing homes. Nursing homes that do not meet standards will face tough penalties.

Finally, the law provides $5 billion to support health insurance coverage offered by employers to their "early retirees"—individuals who retiree at between 55 years of age and less than 65 years of age, the point at which they would be eligible for Medicare. These funds are available until 2014 when a guaranteed source of affordable coverage would become available through new state exchanges.

It will take several years for the new law to go into full effect. As a member of the two Senate committees with oversight of health care, I will be following implementation closely to ensure that this law is working for New Mexico.

New Mexico's seniors deserve the best medical system, with consistently excellent and affordable care. Through these and other critical reforms, the Patient Protection and Affordable Care Act will ensure they have access to such a system.

Periodical Bibliography

The following articles have been selected to supplement the diverse views presented in this chapter.

Reed Abelson — "Awaiting Health Law's Prognosis," *New York Times*, February 2, 2011.

Jonathan Cohn — "How They Did It," *New Republic*, June 10, 2010.

Geoff Colvin — "The Business of Obamacare," *Fortune*, March 21, 2011.

Richard A. Epstein — "Bleak Prospects: How Health Care Reform Has Failed in the United States," *Texas Review of Law and Politics*, Fall 2010.

Jay Herson and David Pearce Snyder — "Health Insurance in America After the Reform," *Futurist*, March-April 2010.

Paul Howard and Stephen T. Parente — "Toward Real Health Care Reform," *National Affairs*, Summer 2010.

Stanley Kurtz — "The Acronym That Ate Health Care," *National Review*, May 16, 2011.

Yuval Levin — "Obamacare's Retreating Defenses," *National Review*, June 6, 2011.

R.R. Reno — "Reforming the Health-Care Reform," *First Things: A Monthly Journal of Religion and Public Life*, June/July 2010.

Steve Riczo — "ObamaCare's Rocky Road to Reality," *USA Today Magazine*, January 2011.

Luiza Ch. Savage — "The New Fight over Obamacare," *Maclean's*, August 23, 2010.

For Further Discussion

Chapter 1

1. After reading the first pair of viewpoints in this chapter, name some positive and negative aspects of American health care. Karen Davis, Cathy Schoen, and Kristof Stremikis claim the US health care system provides less effective care and that Americans are less "well" than their counterparts in other countries. Do you think this assessment is true? What evidence supports your opinion on this matter?

2. While so many Americans seem to be losing health insurance, David Amsden reports on a segment of the population that is choosing to forgo coverage. Reread Amsden's viewpoint and examine some of the reasons these people are opting to live without insurance. Do you think these "young invincibles" have valid reasons for taking the risk? Explain why or why not. Can you suggest a way to extend coverage to these people so that they would accept insurance?

3. What aspects of his proposed Medicare reform does Len M. Nichols think would make it a good model for overall health care reform? Do you agree with his plan? What components of the plan do you think are worthwhile and which are impractical? Explain your opinion on its potential for success.

Chapter 2

1. One common argument in the debate over rising health care costs is to blame health insurers for putting profits over affordability. Reread the viewpoints by Health Care for America NOW and Mark Gimein and then decide whether you think health insurers are fairly or unfairly blamed for the rise in health care costs. Quote evidence from the viewpoints to support your opinions.

2. PR newswire reports that business leaders believe that increases in health care costs are driven by pharmaceutical company operations and profit margins. Sally C. Pipes insists drug companies are not to blame for rising costs because their products prevent and cure illnesses, keeping patients safe from expensive hospital treatment or other acute care. Whose argument do you find more convincing? Explain why, using quotes or statistics from the viewpoints.

3. Each of the viewpoints in this chapter debate the blameworthiness of some proposed contributor to rising health care costs. After looking over all the viewpoints, decide which entity is the most responsible for the steep climb in health care costs. Then propose a method of cutting the costs associated with this culprit.

Chapter 3

1. The first two viewpoints in this chapter debate the issue of universal health care for America. While many other nations have government-sponsored, single-payer health care, the United States does not. Do you think America should adopt universal health care as well? Using the arguments made in these two viewpoints, explain your position on this issue.

2. In opposition to single-payer (universal) health care, many policy analysts contend that the health care system should be governed by competition. That is, a free market in health care would supposedly force providers and insurers to compete for consumer dollars, leading to lower costs and better care. What problems does Joe Flower see in a free-market system? Do you think his complaints are valid, or is Michael F. Cannon correct in assuming that competition will help solve the crisis in health care? Explain your answer by reiterating which conclusions you think are most important in the viewpoints.

3. William J. Reindl claims that consumer-driven health care (i.e., the widespread adoption of health savings accounts and other measures) will help lower health care costs for purchasers. Carol L. Owen counters that such plans are not suited to low-income consumers or patients with chronic diseases, as they cannot keep enough money in their health savings accounts to cover potential expenditures. Whose argument do you think is stronger? What place, if any, do you think consumer-driven health care has in efforts to reform the industry?

Chapter 4

1. Michael Tennant claims that the Patient Protection and Affordable Care Act (PPACA) is ruinous because it puts health care in the hands of the government. Tennant insists that the PPACA could permit the government to regulate the behavior of individuals and compel them to purchase health insurance whether they prefer to or not. After reading the viewpoints by Tennant and President Obama, decide whether you think the PPACA signals too much government intrusion in personal choice or whether this intrusion should be welcomed in order to resolve specific health care problems under the current system. Use quotes and arguments from the viewpoints to support your views.

2. What evidence does Paul Ryan give to advance his argument that the Patient Protection and Affordable Care Act (PPACA) will increase the federal deficit? What evidence do Paul N. Van de Water and James R. Horney provide to make their prediction that the PPACA will not increase the nation's debt? Whose evidence do you find more convincing? Explain why.

3. Reread the viewpoints in this chapter and any others you can find that discuss the content of the Patient Protection and Affordable Care Act (PPACA) and the changes it will make

in the current health care system. Write an essay detailing your opinion of the new law. What advantages or disadvantages does it have? Is it a just law or one that is unconstitutional? Should it be repealed? In addressing all these questions, draw support from the viewpoints.

Organizations to Contact

The editors have compiled the following list of organizations concerned with the issues debated in this book. The descriptions are derived from materials provided by the organizations. All have publications or information available for interested readers. The list was compiled on the date of publication of the present volume; the information provided here may change. Be aware that many organizations take several weeks or longer to respond to inquiries, so allow as much time as possible.

Alliance for Health Reform
1444 Eye Street, NW, Suite 910
Washington, DC 20005-6573
(202) 789-2300
e-mail: info@allhealth.org
website: www.allhealth.org

The Alliance for Health Reform seeks to provide current information about health care reform options to those who lead national debates on this issue. Through its balanced, nonpartisan forums, the group works to achieve the ultimate goal of seeing all Americans with health care plans they can afford that provide them necessary, quality care. Issues addressed by the organization include health reform, the cost of health care, private health insurance, and state health issues. Information about these topics and numerous others can be found on the Alliance for Health Reform website.

America's Agenda: Health Care for All
1025 Connecticut Ave., NW, Suite 907
Washington, DC 20036
(877) 223-7002
website: www.americasagenda.org

America's Agenda creates national health care reform campaigns in an effort to promote universal health care coverage for all Americans. The organization sees the passage of the March 2010 federal health care reform as a major victory and has refocused its efforts on ensuring that the care provided is high quality with limited cost inflation. Information about both federal and state campaigns can be found on the organization's website along with copies of previous news briefs and newsletters about health care reform.

American Enterprise Institute (AEI)
1150 Seventeenth Street, NW
Washington, DC 20036
(202) 862-5800 • fax: (202) 862-7177
website: www.aei.org

AEI is an organization that fosters research by scholars and experts in all areas of public policy in order to address current topics concerning both the United States and the international community. Their research is divided into six focuses—economics, foreign policy and defense, health policy, legal and constitutional issues, politics and public opinion, and social and cultural studies. Within the health policy concentration, AEI scholars advocate for "smarter" health care reform and oppose government-centered, top-down reform like that enacted and promoted by Barack Obama and the Democratic Party. Reports such as *A Better Prescription: AEI Scholars on Realistic Health Reform* can be downloaded from the AEI website along with issues of *The American*, the organization's monthly publication.

American Federation of Labor and Congress of Industrial Organizations (AFL-CIO)
815 16th Street, NW
Washington, DC 20006
website: www.aflcio.org

Created in 1955, AFL-CIO consists of national and international labor unions representing a range of professions including teachers, firefighters, farm workers, health care professionals, and public employees, among others. This centralized organization works to ensure that the rights of America's workers are observed and protected. With regard to health care, the organization believes that currently Medicare and Children's Health are two programs working for the American people, but that Health Savings Accounts and Medicare Prescription Drugs must be reformed to better serve U.S. citizens. The AFL-CIO health care hot alerts page provides information about upcoming health care reform and stories about how health care reform is working for American families today.

Brookings Institution

1775 Massachusetts Ave., NW
Washington, DC 20036
(202) 797-6000
website: www.brookings.edu

The Brookings Institution is a nonprofit, public policy organization. Its scholars research a range of issues affecting the United States and the international community, craft policy suggestions to advance the American government and the lives of its citizens, and create a more secure international community by encouraging increased international cooperation. While the institute recognizes the reform offered by the most recent health care legislation, Brookings experts continue to research the issue and argue that ongoing reform is necessary to create a working health care system. Among other pertinent issues, they focus on Medicare reform in articles such as "Both Democrats and Republicans Must Convince Americans that Medicare Is Unsustainable," and "Next Steps on Medicare Reform Now." These articles and others can be read on the Brookings website.

Cato Institute

1000 Massachusetts Ave., NW

Washington, DC 20001-5403
(202) 842-0200 • fax: (202) 842-3490
website: www.cato.org

Cato is a libertarian think tank that works to advance public policy exemplifying the ideals of individual liberty, limited government, free markets, and peace. In accordance with these views, the Cato position on health care maintains that consumers, not the government, should be in control of their care. Specifically, the organization believes that deregulating the health care industry would assist consumers in finding affordable health insurance. Articles and reports such as "Bad Medicine: A Guide to the Real Costs and Consequences of the New Health Care Law," "The Case for High-Deductible Health Insurance," and "Bankrupt: Entitlements and the Federal Budget," can be found on the Cato website, along with digital copies of Cato publications such as the *Cato Journal, Cato Policy Report*, and *Cato's Letters*.

Center for American Progress (CAP)

1333 H Street, NW, 10th Floor
Washington, DC 20005
(202) 682-1611 • fax (202) 682-1967
website: www.americanprogress.org

The Center for American Progress is a progressive public policy organization dedicated to advancing government policy that provides all citizens the opportunity to achieve the American dream. With regard to health care, the organization has supported the Affordable Care Act and sees it as an important step in ensuring that all Americans have access to quality, affordable health care options. Articles concerning this legislation such as "Better Health Means Better Business," "Health Reform and Employment" and "How Does Health Reform Work" can be read on the CAP website.

Centers for Medicare and Medicaid Services

7500 Security Blvd.

Baltimore, MD 21244-1850
website: www.medicare.gov

Medicare.gov is the official US government website dedicated to providing information to the public about the Medicare program; it is maintained by the Centers for Medicare and Medicaid Services (CMS) agency. The site provides extensive information concerning the program, including Medicare basics and frequently asked questions.

HealthCare.gov
website: www.healthcare.gov

HealthCare.gov is a website launched following the passage of the Affordable Health Care Act. The website's purpose is to explain the law and its impact on Americans, and to provide assistance for individuals in finding appropriate health care options. There is a timeline that shows the changes that will be made to health care coverage through 2015 as well as information about how the legislation will affect certain groups such as veterans, rural Americans, and health care providers. HealthCare Notes is the website's blog with updates on current health care topics and legislation.

Healthcare-NOW!
1315 Spruce Street
Philadelphia, PA 19107
(800) 453-1305
e-mail: info@healthcare-now.org
website: www.healthcare-now.org

Healthcare-NOW! has been working on the grassroots level since its founding in 2004 to advocate for and promote the passage of a publicly funded, single-payer health care system that would provide all Americans with access to quality health care. The organization's website provides information about what a single-payer system would entail. Additionally, facts about current, ongoing, and past campaigns can be found at the website.

The Henry J. Kaiser Family Foundation (KFF)
2400 Sand Hill Road
Menlo Park, CA 94025
(650) 854-9400 • fax (650) 854-4800
website: www.kff.org

KFF is a nonprofit, private organization dedicated to providing information about national health care issues in the United States and asserting the position the country should take in global health care policy issues. The foundation focuses most of its efforts on conducting policy analysis and research, providing a clearinghouse of all health policy related information, and running health information campaigns in the United States and abroad. Most of KFF's work is focused on areas such as health reform, Medicaid/CHIP, Medicare, insurance costs, and coverage for the uninsured, to name a few. Detailed reports about these topics and others can be accessed on the organization's website.

Heritage Foundation
214 Massachusetts Ave., NE
Washington, DC 20002-4999
(202) 546-4400
e-mail: info@heritage.org
website: www.heritage.org

A public policy institute promoting the conservative ideals of free enterprise, limited government, individual freedom, traditional American values, and a strong national defense, Heritage opposes government-run health care. The organization's statement of purpose on the issue argues that the current level of government control has led to decreased personal freedom and limits citizens' ability to make appropriate health care choices that suit their families' needs. The organization's main objective regarding health care reform is to increase the number of individuals who purchase their health insurance directly from a health insurance company. Many of the organization's publications assert the shortcomings of the 2010 reforms and their negative impact on the country and health care. Reports explicating this stance are available on the Heritage website along with numerous others addressing the need for health care reform and private control of the system.

Universal Health Care Action Network (UHCAN)

2800 Euclid Ave., #520
Cleveland, OH 22115-2418
(216) 241-8422 • fax (216) 241-8423
website: www.uhcan.org

UHCAN advocates for health care coverage for all Americans that is both continuous and affordable. UHCAN believes that grassroots organization provides the best method for achieving the political change necessary to enact reform that will ensure this level of care for all. To foster improved local organization, the UHCAN website provides links to numerous websites seeking to achieve similar health care policy goals.

US Department of Health and Human Services (HHS)

200 Independence Ave., SW
Washington, DC 20201
(877) 696-6775
website: www.hhs.gov

HHS is the US government agency charged with ensuring that all Americans have access to quality health care options regardless of their health condition. It is also the agency that heads the Medicare program. Information about this program and others can be found on the HHS website. Further general information about health care and the agency's work can be grouped into topics including prevention, disease, and regulations.

Bibliography of Books

Marcia Angell

The Truth About the Drug Companies: How They Deceive Us and What to Do About It. New York: Random House, 2004.

Donald L. Barlett and James B. Steele

Critical Condition: How Health Care in America Became Big Business—and Bad Medicine. New York: Broadway, 2006.

Donald A. Barr

Health Disparities in the United States: Social Class, Race, Ethnicity, and Health. Baltimore: The Johns Hopkins University Press, 2008.

Shannon Brownlee

Overtreated: Why Too Much Medicine Is Making Us Sicker and Poorer. New York: Bloomsbury USA, 2007.

Clayton M. Christensen, Jerome H. Grossman, and Jason Hwang

The Innovator's Prescription: A Disruptive Solution for Health Care. New York: McGraw-Hill, 2009.

Jonathan Cohn

Sick: The Untold Story of America's Health Care Crisis—and the People Who Pay the Price. New York: HarperCollins, 2008.

Tom Daschle with Scott S. Greenberger and Jeanne M. Lambrew

Critical: What We Can Do About the Health-Care Crisis. New York: Thomas Dunne, 2008.

Steven M. Davidson	*Still Broken: Understanding the U.S. Health Care System.* Stanford, CA: Stanford University Press, 2010.
Peter Ferrara	*The Obamacare Disaster.* Chicago: Heartland Institute, 2010.
David Gratzer	*Why Obama's Government Takeover of Health Care Will Be a Disaster.* New York: Encounter, 2009.
George C. Halvorson	*Health Care Will Not Reform Itself: A User's Guide to Refocusing and Reforming American Health Care.* New York: Productivity, 2009.
Regina E. Herzlinger	*Who Killed Health Care?: America's $2 Trillion Medical Problem—and the Consumer-Driven Cure.* New York: McGraw-Hill, 2007.
Lawrence R. Jacobs and Theda Skocpol	*Health Care Reform and American Politics: What Everyone Needs to Know.* New York: Oxford University Press, 2010.
Steven Jonas, Raymond Goldsteen, and Karen Goldsteen	*An Introduction to the U.S. Health Care System.* New York: Springer, 2007.
Maggie Mahar	*Money-Driven Medicine: The Real Reason Health Care Costs So Much.* New York: Collins, 2006.
David Nather	*The New Health Care System: Everything You Need to Know.* New York: Thomas Dunne, 2010.

Sally C. Pipes — *The Truth About Obamacare.* Washington, DC: Regnery, 2010.

Michael E. Porter and Elizabeth Olmsted Teisberg — *Redefining Health Care: Creating Value-Based Competition on Results.* Boston: Harvard Business School Press, 2006.

T.R. Reid — *The Healing of America: A Global Quest for Better, Cheaper, and Fairer Health Care.* New York: Penguin, 2010.

Grace-Marie Turner, James C. Capretta, Thomas P. Miller, and Robert E. Moffitt — *Why ObamaCare Is Wrong for America: How the New Health Care Law Drives Up Costs, Puts Government in Charge of Your Decisions, and Threatens Your Constitutional Rights.* New York: Broadside, 2011.

The Washington Post Staff — *Landmark: The Inside Story of America's New Health Care Law and What It Means for Us All.* New York: Public Affairs, 2010.

Carol S. Weissert and William G. Weissert — *Governing Health: The Politics of Health Policy.* Baltimore: The Johns Hopkins University Press, 1996.

Index

measures for, 25, 31
at no cost, 205
promoting care, 120–121
screenings, 62
PricewaterhouseCoopers survey, 106
Prostate-specific antigen (PSA) test, 62, 125

Q

Quality health care, 25–47, 58, 144
Quality of life, 56–57

R

RAND Health Insurance Experiment, 166, 191
Regence BlueShield of Idaho, 109
Reindl, William J., 181–188
Rollins School of Public Health, 129
Rother, John, 90, 95
Ryan, Paul, 88, 97, 205, 223–229, 231

S

Safe care, 31–38
Schoen, Cathy, 22–58
School-based health centers, 216
Schulze, Nichole, 77
Schwarzenegger, Arnold, 82
Sekhar, Sonia, 116–126
Serota, Scott P., 111
Service Employees International Union, 195
Sicko (film), 163
Single-payer system, 134–135
Smith, Ryan, 203
Social Security, 87, 90, 98, 228–229, 232
Social Security Act (1935), 149
Socialized medicine, 134, 212–213
Spinal cord injury, 119, 123–124, 155

State Children's Health Insurance Program (S-CHIP), 156, 191
Stremikis, Kristof, 22–58
Strokes, 129
Summers, Larry, 159
Sustainable growth rate (SGR), 234–236, 243
Sweden, health care, 142
Switzerland, health care, 142

T

Tallon, James R., 76, 80
Tax breaks
for employer-sponsored care, 167
reforming, 163–165
for small businesses, 205–207
tax rates for, 192
Tennant, Michael, 210–222
Thoma, Mark, 17
Thompson, Art, 211–212, 220–221
Thompson, Michael, 106
Thorpe, Kenneth, 129
Timeliness of care, 43, 47
Tonik, 78

U

Unemployment rates, 70, 156
Uninsured Americans
access to health care, 156
equity measures, 56
free-market help for, 172–173
health care costs, 224–225
incurring debt, 81–83
invincible attitudes by, 83–84
number of, 15
substandard care for, 79–81
United Hospital Fund, 76, 80
United Kingdom, health care
access to care, 155
chronic care, 31
continuity and feedback measures, 42